Guiding
PROFESSIONAL
LEARNING
COMMUNITIES

*We remain profoundly grateful to the body of
rigorous researchers who have conducted the carefully designed studies of
professional learning communities (PLCs) in schools in order to identify
the characteristics of effective PLCs—what they look like and how they act—in
order to push classroom practice to higher levels of quality so that all students
learn, and learn well. They have provided the grist with which to initiate
and launch PLCs in schools. In addition, they have articulated tough questions
about the when, where, how of PLCs and have called attention to the need
for substantive, intentional learning by the PLC members. Their work has
guided our practice, and to them we dedicate this volume.*

*To the risk-taking school leaders and their staffs who, with courage and
probably some trepidation, engaged their campus practitioners in the learning
work of the PLC, we are deeply appreciative. Their stories of pressure,
persuasion, support, encouragement, and wheedling and needling have
informed us of the trials and tribulations and of the triumphs and rewards of
PLC schools where students benefit from the staff's continuous learning—the
result for which we all strive. Thank you for continuing to raise the flag and
march to the drum of the PLC beat today and, we hope, for years to come. We
dedicate this book to you, the practitioner, who takes the many theories found in
education and grinds them into flour so they become the bread that
sustains and nourishes all that is good in learning.*

*Finally, we dedicate this book to children. First, our own children who have
inspired us to rise above ourselves and to give our talents and gifts to make the
world a better place: Bruce; Melissa, Mark, and Matt; and Temple and Perry.
But, importantly, also to the children of the world, who as John W. Whitehead
reminds us "are the living messages we send to a time we will not see." Our work
is, ultimately, for the children.*

Shirley M. Hord

James L. Roussin

William A. Sommers

Guiding PROFESSIONAL LEARNING COMMUNITIES

Inspiration, Challenge, Surprise, and Meaning

Shirley M. Hord | **James L. Roussin** | **William A. Sommers**

Foreword by Roland S. Barth

CORWIN
A SAGE Company

For information:

Corwin
A SAGE Company
2455 Teller Road
Thousand Oaks, California 91320
(800) 233-9936
Fax: (800) 417-2466
www.corwinpress.com

SAGE Ltd.
1 Oliver's Yard
55 City Road
London EC1Y 1SP
United Kingdom

SAGE Pvt. Ltd.
B 1/I 1 Mohan Cooperative
   Industrial Area
Mathura Road, New Delhi 110 044
India

SAGE Asia-Pacific Pte. Ltd.
33 Pekin Street #02-01
Far East Square
Singapore 048763

Printed in the United States of America

Library of Congress Cataloging-in-Publication Data

Hord, Shirley M.
Guiding professional learning communities : inspiration, challenge, surprise, and meaning/ Shirley M. Hord, James L. Roussin, William A. Sommers ; foreword by Roland S. Barth.
       p. cm.
Includes bibliographical references and index.
ISBN 978-1-4129-7271-0 (pbk.)

   1. School improvement programs—United States. 2. Group work in education—United States. 3. Educational change—United States. 4. Educational leadership—United States. I. Roussin, James L. II. Sommers, William A. III. Title.

LB2822.82.H666 2010
371.2′03—dc22   2009035694

This book is printed on acid-free paper.

09 10 11 12 13 10 9 8 7 6 5 4 3 2 1

Acquisitions Editor:	Dan Alpert
Associate Editor:	Megan Bedell
Production Editor:	Veronica Stapleton
Copy Editor:	Alison Hope
Typesetter:	C&M Digitals (P) Ltd.
Proofreader:	Susan Schon
Indexer:	Jean Casalegno
Cover Designer:	Rose Storey

Contents

Foreword

Roland S. Barth

In a few days, I will be leading a workshop on professional learning communities (PLCs) for a school district here along the Maine coast. I find that the pages I have just read—and the pages you are about to read—have admirably "staff developed" me for the task.

Why? Because in this tidy little volume I have found a valuable companion piece to the authors' earlier *Leading Professional Learning Communities.* You will find here a resource and workbook for those who would both create and strengthen their PLCs. Unlike most resource books, this one offers not only precisely-targeted readings but also an abundance of detailed and inventive activity plans that can take school leaders a long way toward constructing staff development activities low on "sit 'n git" and high on involvement, engagement, and learning. With these plans, staff members will simultaneously engage in their own learning and contribute to the learning of others.

In short, using the tools offered here, leaders of adult learning will model and demonstrate as well as teach what a professional learning community is all about. The activities promise to help embed in schools a culture of continuous professional learning.

But the skeptical part of me, born from years within the schoolhouse, reacts differently to this PLC business. Whoa! Is the professional learning community concept yet another "bandwagon"? During my half century as an educator, I have been around, been aboard (not to mention run over by), and led what seems like a never ending wagon train of new ideas and solutions to the knotty, recurring issues confronting schools: SMSG Mathematics, open education, team teaching, non-graded instruction, total quality management, principal centers. Remember them? Many turned out to be fads and were abandoned by the wayside. Others took root and continue to flourish. But the plethora of bandwagons has left all too many education professionals feeling betrayed, cynical, and wary of what will come down the pike next. No one wants to be run over again.

And now, along come professional learning communities, or PLCs as they are popularly known. Educators have seized upon the tenets of PLCs— or had them inflicted upon them—and have jumped aboard this latest bandwagon.

Or is it a bandwagon?

There are probably as many different conceptions of PLCs as there are advocates and opponents. As I understand the concept, and as the authors so elegantly present it, a PLC is a school culture that enhances teacher quality through the intentional, collegial instruction of all educators for the purpose of promoting student learning. The compelling belief is that profound learning for teachers begets profound learning for students.

Researchers have long sought the holy grail of school characteristics that are positively correlated with exceptional student learning. And they have identified many candidates for consideration, including class size, rigorous curriculum, educational background of teachers, new buildings and facilities, and the leadership of the principal, among others. Yet no characteristic has more influence on pupil learning and has proved, through research, more durable over time than quality of teaching. I suspect it will in the future as well.

A laser-like focus on quality teaching for the purpose of promoting student learning is the hallmark of professional learning communities. Skeptical as I may be, I am confident that *this* "new idea" is not really new at all. Nor will it become an abandoned fad. To be sure, the nomenclature may change over the years, but the links between a culture of professional learning for educators, quality teaching, and profound learning for youngsters will endure. If PLCs constitute the latest bandwagon, I say, "It's about time."

So how do we, as a profession, move from the worthy goals driving PLCs to powerful adult and student learning? Here lies the contribution of this book, which focuses in great detail on *how* to pull it off. Here you will find abundant "learning opportunities" for educators, which closely link this incontrovertibly good idea with practice. Providing explicit, vivid activities hospitable to teachers' and administrators' learning alike, this book is a kind of user's guide to professional learning communities. I am confident that a good read will admirably prepare you, as it has me, to lead the way. Enjoy!

Acknowledgments

This manuscript has been a team effort—not only among the authors, but also with others from whom we gained intellectual stamina, consistent help and support, and a sense of urgency.

We are especially indebted to Leslie Ash Blair, University of Texas at Austin—good friend, special colleague, and editor extraordinaire. She has received our incomplete sentences, comma blunders, grammatical atrocities, and paragraph crazies. Out of these, she produced whole cloth: weaving in understanding, insight, and significant intellectual messages.

Dan Alpert, Corwin Press, has remained our ever-constant and stalwart friend and advisor throughout the process, not only of the "mother" book, but also of this offspring volume. He walked "beside us" to our everlasting appreciation and delight.

Nancy Reynolds, Information Specialist at Southwest Educational Development Laboratory, was the special sleuth who tracked elusive references and citations, in addition to accessing those pesky permissions, always needed, and always challenging to writers to acquire.

The leadership of the National Staff Development Council has been part of this endeavor: various members have made suggestions, offered critiques, and supported the production of this material to guide the communities of professional learners in schools, who through their continuous learning become ever-increasingly effective in providing quality teaching that results in ever-growing numbers of successful student learners.

A most hearty thank you to all.

About the Authors

**Shirley M. Hord, PhD,** is scholar laureate associated with the National Staff Development Council, following her retirement as Scholar Emerita at the Southwest Educational Development Laboratory in Austin, Texas. There she directed the Strategies for Increasing Student Success Program. She continues to monitor the Leadership for Change Project, and support applications of the Concerns-Based Adoption Model (CBAM). In addition, she designs and coordinates professional development activities related to educational change, school improvement, and school leadership.

Her early roles as elementary school classroom teacher and university science education faculty at The University of Texas at Austin were followed by her appointment as codirector of Research on the Improvement Process at the Research and Development Center for Teacher Education at The University of Texas at Austin. There she administered and conducted research on school improvement and the role of school leadership in school change. This work focused on the concerns and needs of teachers implementing change in their content knowledge and instructional practices, and how leaders support them through structures and staff development interventions during the change process.

She served as a fellow of the National Center for Effective Schools Research and Development and was U.S. representative to the Foundation for the International School Improvement Project, an international effort that develops research, training, and policy initiatives to support local school improvement practices.

In addition to working with educators at all levels across the U.S. and Canada, Hord makes presentations and consults in Asia, Europe, Australia, Africa, and Mexico.

Her current interests focus on qualitative research into understanding and delivering comprehensive educational reform to schools, and the functioning and creation of educational organizations as learning communities and the role of leaders who serve such organizations. Dr. Hord is the author of numerous articles and books, the most recent of which are

Implementing Change: Patterns, Principles, and Potholes (3rd edition; with Gene E. Hall)

Learning Together, Leading Together: Changing Schools Through Professional Learning Communities (editor)

Leading Professional Learning Communities: Voices from Research and Practice (2008).

James L. Roussin has been committed to improving teaching and learning in schools across the United States and abroad for the past 26 years. He has worked as a language arts teacher; gifted coordinator; ESL coordinator; curriculum director; executive director of teaching, learning, and school improvement; adjunct professor; and educational consultant.

Roussin is currently working as a strategic change consultant, and is the executive director for *Generative Human Systems.*

Roussin helped to revitalize the Minnesota Staff Development Council from 1998 to 2004 and served as its president for four of those years. He is currently serving as a board trustee on the National Staff Development Council.

He is a teaching associate for Human Systems Dynamics (an institute that is using complexity theory to impact organizational development work). He is also a national trainer for leadership development, cognitive coaching, adaptive schools, QLD (quality leadership by design)—S.M.A.R.T. goals, and program evaluation.

In February of 2006, Roussin traveled to India on a Berkana Learning Journey to explore new forms of leadership that are emerging in global communities. More recently, he spent four months working in the Middle East with ASCD-Middle East in supporting the Ministry of Education in implementing new teacher development standards.

Roussin's current interests focus on healthy organizations and human development through the lens of natural systems theory and complexity science.

James L. Roussin is certified as a coach and facilitator in the following areas:

Neurosomatic and Meta-Coach

Integral Coaching—New Ventures West

Cognitive Coaching

Appreciative Coaching

Symbolic Modeling & Clean Language Coaching

Human Systems Dynamics Associate—Complexity Science and Organizational Development

Adaptive Schools

Conflict to Consensus Facilitator

Program Evaluation

 **William A. Sommers, PhD**, of Austin, Texas, is currently the director of Learning Alternatives and is leadership coach for Spring Lake Park District 16 in Spring Lake Park, Minnesota. He is also a consultant and author. He is the former director of Leadership & Organizational Development for Manor Independent School District in Texas, the former executive director for secondary curriculum and professional learning for Minneapolis Public Schools, and has been a school administrator for more than 30 years. He has been a senior fellow for the Urban Leadership Academy at the University of Minnesota. Sommers also has served as an adjunct faculty member at Texas State University, Hamline University, University of St. Thomas, St. Mary's University, Union Institute, and Capella University.

Sommers was on the board of Trustees for five years and Past-President for the National Staff Development Council. He has been a presenter in preconferences and conference sessions for 12 consecutive years and continues to work as a senior consultant for NSDC.

Since 1990, he has been an associate trainer for the Center for Cognitive Coaching based in Denver, Colorado. He has been a program director for an adolescent chemical dependency treatment center and on the board of a halfway house for 20 years.

Sommers has co-authored seven books:

Living on a Tightrope: A Survival Handbook for Principals

Trainer's Companion: Stories to Stimulate Conversation, Reflection, and Action

Becoming a Successful Principal: How to Ride the Wave of Change Without Drowning

Reflective Practice to Improve Schools: A Trainer's Companion

Energizing Staff Development Using Video Clips

Leading Professional Learning Communities

Principal's Field Manual

He is currently working on a trainer's companion for *Habits of Mind* (Costa and Kallick, 2009) with his coauthor Walter (Skip) Olsen.

In addition to writing many articles regarding coaching, assessment, and reflective thinking, he also does training in reflective practice, leadership, organizational development, conflict management, poverty, thinking skills, brain research, and classroom management. From 1970 to the present he has been in K–12 education as a teacher and principal in urban, suburban, and rural schools. Sommers is a practitioner who integrates theory into the learning opportunities he facilitates.

Part I

Introduction

Things You Need to Know Before You Use This Book

Thank you for taking the opportunity to read this book, a companion to *Leading Professional Learning Communities: Voices from Research and Practice.* No one volume can provide the abundance of information and material required for the development and implementation of an effective PLC, whether on a school campus, at the district level, or at other sites. We hope this book will provide you with useful tools, resources, and insights as you and your team create and implement a PLC.

For this second book, we have partnered with James L. Roussin (please see About The Authors to learn more about Roussin). We have gained much insight from James L. Roussin's observations, broad reading, and study of the literature; interactions with school leaders and staffs; wisdom; and critical thinking. We believe his significant contributions will be valuable to you and your team as you engage in the often difficult, but extremely rewarding, work needed to become a PLC.

WHAT IS A PLC?

There are many educators across the United States who describe the PLC in their school as the third-grade team meeting (or other grades in the elementary school) or math department meeting (or other academic subject matter departments in the secondary school)—period. There appears to be no further description of why the participants meet, nor what they do when they assemble. As you will recall from the first volume, we were very clear about two issues, and we revisit them here before we begin.

WHO ARE THE MEMBERS OF THE PLC?

We believe that the school is best served when two organizational arrangements are established within a PLC. The first of these is the grade-level team (in the elementary school) or subject-matter team (in the secondary school), in which the educators address and resolve issues concerning their particular grade level or department subject-matter curriculum, their specific students' needs, and the appropriate instructional strategies that best serve these students. In this setting, the teachers and administrators involved will undertake appropriate study and learning about these issues in order to become more effective in meeting their students' needs, thereby increasing student learning and success.

There is a second and important arrangement of the professionals in the school for the PLC. In this structure, all professionals at the school come together to meet as one community—comprising all staff members of the school—to share what the smaller units are learning and to carry out the specific learning that the whole school group deems important. This creates the environment for working on the school's common purpose, and for directing the adults' learning toward the school goals. Without this larger group's collegial and intentional learning, the various parts of the staff are moving in different directions that may well result in the lack of alignment of the scope and sequence of student learning.

WHY ESTABLISH AND SUPPORT PLC IN A SCHOOL?

In brief, the PLC centers on *quality teaching* that results in students' successful learning. Quality teaching is strengthened and increased through continuous professional learning, and the PLC setting promotes this adult learning. Because understanding the purpose of a PLC is foundational to its creation and support, the first activity of this field book creates a short rationale for operating as a PLC.

Make no mistake: our primary focus is the learning and teaching that occurs in the school. Only by increasing the effectiveness of teaching quality, which results in higher student outcomes, are PLCs made to be worthwhile. Without this goal as its imperative, a PLC will be just another failed program.

A key reason for writing this follow-up volume was to provide additional support for implementing PLCs, through a series of learning opportunities for the PLC participants' engagement. Teams often struggle if learning opportunities are unstructured. The opportunities presented here provide structure and direct discussion and thinking in ways that help teams focus on student learning, as well as their own learning. Thus, this book takes readers deeper into the implementation of PLCs by facilitating individual and group development and growth.

WHY THIS BOOK?

We think of this book as an overview, or a compendium, of learnings that would benefit individuals who are just launching a PLC, or for those who have been "in the trenches" for some time. We believe that the material will appeal to both the PLC initiate and to the sophisticate. The material ranges from the mundane to the metaphysical to reach a wide array of stakeholders. It will ask participants to respond to or engage in the process of learning in order to respond to such questions as the following:

Where can we find time for PLC?

How am I being asked to stretch or grow in my work for students, for my life, my leadership?

Who or what at this time is inspiring me in my life to become more than I am now?

What has surprised me about my work in schools, my leadership, myself? How do I make room for the unexpected?

Where do I find myself deeply touched or moved by my colleagues, my students, my experiences?

How do we increase reflection on our practice, design more effective actions to be used in the classroom, and distribute this "intelligence" internally and externally throughout the system?

How Will This Book Complement Leading PLCs?

The previous book written by Shirley Hord and William Sommers—*Leading Professional Learning Communities: Voices from Research and Practice*—was created to describe and provide rich content about the research-based components of a PLC, the significant role of leaders, measures for assessing the degree to which the PLC is functioning effectively, as well as other topics. The key words for the first book are *description* and *content;* the first book is about *the what.*

The new book addresses the *process,* or *how to* launch, develop, create, and implement a PLC in the school—in other words, how to put the content of the first book into practice. Could the books be used independently of each other? Obviously, if the individual is interested in simply knowing about PLCs, then the first book is sufficient. However, we realized upon completion of the original book that, while it served a valuable purpose in identifying the research base about PLCs and providing examples in schools, it would be insufficient for helping busy practitioners go about the challenging tasks of creating PLC in their own schools. Hence, this book.

Is the second book useful without the first? Certainly, it could be, but only if the user recognizes that the major purpose of PLCs is to increase and enhance teaching quality through the collegial intentional learning of educators. It appears that many school leaders view the PLC as an opportunity for teachers to meet, without apparent identification of purpose. The PLC purpose is to support the learning of administrators and teachers in order for them to increase their effectiveness, and, thus, increase the successful learning of students.

How Is This Book Organized?

The remainder of this book comprises three parts:

Part II: Words to the Wise

Part III: Learning Opportunities

Part IV: Bringing Closure

We suggest that your group complete Learning Opportunity 0.1 (A Crisp Rationale for PLCs), Learning Opportunity 0.2 (Benefits to Staff and Students: A Flamingo Dialogue), and Learning Opportunity 0.3 (Research-Based Components for a PLC: A Jigsaw) before moving on to any other learning opportunities. These first three learning opportunities provide the understanding of what a true PLC is. They are necessary to fully develop the dimensions necessary for a PLC.

Part II

Words to the Wise

Before You Begin

As you begin to use the learning opportunities in this book, we would like to focus on several aspects of PLCs. First, we think creating and maintaining PLCs is vital. Second, understanding the research-based components of effective PLCs is essential to the creation of new PLCs. Third, there is research that identifies the benefits to both staff and students when a school staff is organized in a PLC. Thus, we include these concepts as the first three learning opportunities and strongly encourage that your group take advantage of these learning opportunities before moving forward.

TIPS FOR WORKING IN GROUPS

You may want to give a quick glance to some strategies and practices that over the years we have found contribute to the success of our work with groups when conducting professional learning. The ideas are not presented entirely randomly, although there is no real—except for sense-making—order to them.

- Arrange for participants to be seated around tables, so that they may interact, engage in conversation, and process information meaningfully, gaining from the sharing of the group's ideas. We develop understanding and add to our knowledge base more meaningfully and deeply when in a social context (Vygotsky, 1978). We have, in our past, thought we clearly explained to individuals hosting professional learning about this need, only to find ourselves standing before a group in a theatre setting, all facing the front. This requires some creative invention to make it possible for the participants to learn with each other. Thus, we always arrive at our learning session site early and have been known to reorganize the furniture (if it is not bolted down), or ask the participants to reorganize the furniture so the room is conducive to group interaction. 'Nuff said here.

- You will find in a couple of the learning opportunities a suggestion for inviting participants to number themselves around their tables. This gives each person a "name" by which the session leader may invite them to facilitate the group's conversation. This is simply an efficient means of identifying a person to do this, and rotating the facilitation around the group. We used to suggest that the facilitator be the person who had the latest haircut (or some such other trivial identification), which was all informal and fun, but took too much of the learning time for the group to figure out who this person is.

- We like to "invite" the participants to engage in the various activities that have been designed for their learning. That is, we avoid language such as "I want you to," which sounds more directive and less collaborative.

We would also like to remind you that the leader conducting the learning session is not "a potted plant." That is, this person is not rooted in front of the participants with a PowerPoint presentation, alternately flipping a slide on the screen and lecturing, then moving on to the next slide and its accompanying lecture. Sometimes we have seen the slide-lecture scheme interrupted by having the participants chat with their neighbor about the topic. The participants' learning is entirely based on what the leader shares or what neighbors may add. What can the participants take away with them? Do they have some text or material provided so that they might refer to it later, process it with neighbor colleagues, and begin to internalize the content?

What does the research say about how adults, and children, learn? The Joyce and Showers (2002) model provides the steps in what is needed for good professional development. These steps, briefly, are as follows:

- **Tell**
- **Demonstrate** or model
- **Give** opportunity to practice
- **Provide** feedback on the practice
- **Follow up** and coaching

We would like to reiterate here the importance of Vygotsky (1978) and constructivist learning. And although the work of Joyce and Showers and Vygotsky have been discussed and written about for thirty years now, we continue to see an abundance of "stand up and tell" professional development. Ugh . . .

As Confucius said,

Tell me, I'll forget.

Show me, I may remember.

Involve me, and I'll understand.

The learning opportunities in this book involve staff members in their own learning. They are meant to support the facilitator in developing a process for the deep learning of the community. If they are used in a superficial way, however, the results will be diminished. And, what do the professionals learn? Their learning is related directly to the needs of their students in order to increase teaching quality and the successful learning of students.

This means that the professionals will examine multiple sources of student data to identify areas where students are performing successfully and areas that require teaching attention. When a priority area for attention has been identified, the professionals determine what they will revise or change in their teaching practices that will enable students to learn well. Subsequently, professional learning is specified that will develop the capacity of the professionals to use the new practice in an effective way. Learning to use the new practices effectively requires ongoing, substantive, and job-embedded professional development or learning. These steps are the focus of attention in the PLC and are given attention in Learning Opportunity 3.4 (The Learning Community's Work) and Learning Opportunity 3.5 (Identifying a PLC Learning Goal). It is understood that these activities that comprise the PLC's work should be supported by the district or larger organization through resources, policy, leadership, and a culture that values school change and improvement that is based on the continuous learning of the professionals.

Part III

Learning Opportunities

Tools, Tasks, Deep Thinking, and a Wee Bit of Trivia

This section contains numerous opportunities for the leaders and the participants of the PLC to become powerful learners. The opportunities provide tools and tasks that help participants learn content, strategies, techniques, and approaches for improving the operation of their PLC, and for improving classroom instruction. These opportunities derive from ideas found in the research and stories of successful PLCs, and from the authors' activities in supporting PLCs in their development. The learning opportunities have been tested, though not all through rigorous research and evaluation, but they have been used in real schools and classrooms with real administrators and real teachers in real time.

Each learning opportunity contains the following parts:

- The outcome of the learning opportunity
- The assumptions that explain why we think this learning opportunity is important
- A suggestion of the amount of time required for introducing and using this opportunity with one's PLC
- A list of materials needed for the activity
- A step-by-step set of directions for using the activity
- An example of a future application task that the participants will be asked to do

Any text material (research and journal papers, articles, or book excerpts) is appended to the Learning Opportunity for the leaders' and participants' use.

LEARNING OPPORTUNITY 0.1

A Crisp Rationale for PLCs

The test of the morality of a society is what it does for its children.

—Dietrich Bonhoeffer

Outcome

Learners will explain concisely and clearly to others why PLCs are vital to improving schools.

Assumption

We believe a precise understanding of why a PLC can be a useful structure in the school or district is vital to the development and implementation of a PLC.

Suggested Time

20–30 minutes

Materials

- "WHY Worksheet" (see p. 13; one copy for each participant)

Learning Event

1. **Organize** participants around tables so that they may interact with each other. Make certain each person has a worksheet, then ask each table group to number their members around the table, beginning with 1, 2, and so on. This is a shortcut to be able to invite an individual at the table to serve as a facilitator of the conversation later during this session.

2. **Set the stage** by asking participants to write on the back, blank side of their worksheet one statement indicating why or why not PLCs are vital to improving our schools. Solicit responses.

3. **Point out** that the handout has space for responses to four questions that serve as the focus of this learning opportunity. As you will see, each question below will be the focus of small group discussions.

   o **Question 1.** What is the purpose of schools? Alternatively, what is the bottom line reason that we have schools? Person #1 at each table will facilitate a 2-minute conversation with the table group, so each group collectively determines a response using no more than four words.

(The leader will "tour the tables" to eavesdrop on the conversations.)

After 2 minutes, the leader will signal the small groups for their attention. The leader will suggest that people all over the world indicate that the reason for schools is "student learning. You may have discussed *what* students are to learn, or *how* they will learn it, or *where*, but do you agree that student learning is the purpose of schools?" Heads should nod affirmatively.

o **Question 2.** If the purpose of schools is student learning, what is the most significant factor in whether students learn well? Person #2 at your table, please facilitate a 2-minute conversation so the members determine a three-word response.

(Leader, tour the tables.)

Signal for the attention of the whole group after 2 minutes. Again, the leader suggests that almost all people say that the most significant factor in whether students learn well is "quality teaching. We did not say quality *teachers*, but *quality teaching*. After all, nearly all of the personnel in the building contribute to the quality of teaching that students receive. Does this make sense?"

o **Question 3.** If the purpose of schools is student learning, and teaching quality is the most significant factor in student learning, how can quality teaching be enhanced, increased, improved? Invite person #3 to facilitate the discussion that results in a response of no more than three words.

As above, gather attention after 2 minutes, and report, "If the purpose of schools is student learning, and teaching quality is the most significant factor in student learning, quality teaching can be enhanced through *continuous professional learning.*" Invite agreement again.

o **Question 4.** By whom, with what, and how is continuous learning most fruitfully achieved? Three words (*community*, *professionals*, and *learning*) are printed under Line 4 of the WHY Worksheet. Ask person #4 to conduct a conversation with his or her table group that defines what those words mean. Give 3 minutes for this activity, then reconvene the large group and solicit meanings, which should contain content as follows (Hord & Hirsh, 2008, p. 24):

Professionals—Who will participate in the PLC? Answer: those staff in the school who have the responsibility and accountability to deliver an effective instructional program to students, ensuring that students achieve high standards of learning. PLCs include teachers, administrators, and instructional support staff (who are counselors, librarians, school psychologists, etc.).

Learning—What will dominate the work of the PLC? Answer: the needs of the professionals are paramount—the content and activities, the knowledge and skills that they feel are necessary to support improved instructional practice and to increase their effectiveness. The PLC is structured around adults learning so they develop the competencies required to ensure successful student learning.

Community—How is learning structured and organized to support educators in advancing their knowledge and skills? Answer: the staff comes together in a group, exhibiting the characteristics of community, such as democratic participation. The community is organized to provide the structures and processes to leverage the benefit of adult collegial learning.

4. **Ask** the groups to consider the points that have been made during this learning event. They are to imagine themselves as a small committee that is before the school board, in an effort to convince the board of the value of implementing PLCs and to request the provision of time and resources for creating and maintaining PLCs in their buildings. They should create a brief list of talking points, considering that they will have only 10 minutes for their presentation, followed by 5 minutes for board questions.

5. **Provide closure** by inviting the groups to share their work with all, and how—and if—this learning opportunity has provided clarity and conciseness to their views of PLC. Invite commentary regarding the strong points that were heard.

Future Application

Review the work of the learning opportunity with your colleagues at a staff or PLC meeting at your school. Review the rationale and suggestions for a school board presentation. Using this as a draft, create talking points and a presentation for the parent association at your school. Parents will need to be aware of the initiation of the PLC and how it can contribute to their students' learning, most especially if the implementation of a PLC is related to any change in the school's schedules.

Notes:

PROFESSIONAL LEARNING COMMUNITIES WHY WORKSHEET

With your table colleagues, please answer, restricting your answers to two to five words.

1.

2.

3.

4.

Definitions

Community

Professionals

Learning

LEARNING OPPORTUNITY 0.2

Benefits to Staff and to Students: A Flamingo Dialogue

A clay pot sitting in the sun will always be a clay pot. It has to go through the white heat of the furnace to become porcelain.

—Mildred Witte Stoven

Outcome

Learners will articulate the outcomes or benefits for staff and for students derived from PLCs.

Assumption

If the PLC does not add value and increased learning for students, there is not much purpose in creating this arrangement. The theory of change to which we subscribe is that the professionals in the school must be knowledgeable and skilled at their most effective level so that all students learn successfully to high quality standards. Thus, continuous professional learning can contribute to desirable results for the adults, and subsequently to the students.

Please note to participants that they will conduct a "flamingo dialogue"—a short, interactive conversation, lasting as long as they can stand on one foot. Well, not literally—it is just a colorful way to tell them that they will stand for this activity and that it will be brief.

Participants will pair up and move about the room for this activity. Make sure there is space for this.

Suggested Time

30–45 minutes

Materials

- Excerpt from "Professional Learning Communities: What Are They and Why Are They Important?" (use pp. 24–25 in this book; one copy for each participant)
- pp. 18–21 of *Leading Professional Learning Communities: Voices From Research and Practice* (Hord & Sommers, 2008)

Learning Event

1. **Set the stage** by asking participants to reflect on the following question: What are your hunches about how the PLC contributes to your learning, and subsequently to your teaching practices? Tell them to be prepared to share one idea. Ask volunteers to share their reflections.

2. **Invite** participants to organize themselves into dyads, or pairs. They might pair with those who have similar hunches with regard to PLCs or they could pair with those who do not think like they do. Provide each pair with the two pieces of text. They will now decide in their pair who will study the material on staff benefits and who will study the material on students. The participants now read, study, then teach their colleague what they have read. The session leader could call time for the first sharing and invite the second sharing to begin.

3. **After sharing** with each other, ask each pair to converse and develop an explanation of the relationship between the staff benefits and the student benefits. Invite each pair to share their ideas with the larger group.

4. **Provide closure** by asking individuals to return to their larger table groups, and with those colleagues, develop a short (10-minute) presentation to their local newspaper journalist who covers educational issues. They should make a list of talking points that they will use during their presentation. Each table group shares their points with the group. These lists could be collected and reproduced and shared with all table groups.

Future Application

These lists from all the tables could be used periodically by PLCs to remind themselves of the benefits for themselves and their students. Use it as a "booster" shot when the PLC becomes discouraged. A PLC could also use the lists to compare their own outcomes with those on the lists—in other words, the PLC could use the list to check on how their PLC compares to the "ideal."

Notes:

LEARNING OPPORTUNITY 0.3

Research-Based Components of a PLC: A Jigsaw

The greatest discovery of my generation is that human beings can alter their lives by altering their attitudes of mind.

—William James

Outcome

Learners will describe the components or attributes found in the research that characterize effective PLCs.

Assumption

Many voices cite a variety of definitions or dimensions of PLCs. We believe that referring to the research to learn what effective PLCs do is instructive, and using that research is our best bet to create a PLC that is a powerful structure for educators' learning, which in turn influences students' learning.

The time spent on this event could be separated into two parts, dividing and using the two papers, each in one of the 2 hours. The location and space for this learning should be such that the participants are able to move around a bit, because there is a jigsaw activity included.

Suggested Time

1–2 hours.

Materials

- "Imagine," aka "Learn in Community With Others" (see p. 18; one copy for each participant)
- "Professional Learning Communities: What Are They And Why Are They Important?" (see p. 20; one copy for each participant)
- The facilitator will need to review and have on hand *Leading Professional Learning Communities: Voices From Research and Practice* (Hord & Sommers, 2008)
- Flip-chart paper and highlighters

Learning Event

1. **Set the stage** by asking participants to identify one significant attribute of PLCs, then "tour" the group, posting their responses on flip-chart paper.

2. **Organize** participants around tables so that they may interact. Provide each person with "Imagine." Ask them individually to read the article and highlight or underline

three compelling sentences that "speak" to them about professional learning. Provide 8–9 minutes of work time. (The session leader will tour the room to note if groups need more time.)

3. **Ask** person #5 at each table (See Learning Opportunity 0.1, A Crisp Rationale for PLCs, on p. 10) to support the group in a conversation that will result in their identification of one compelling sentence on which they all agree. Give 5 minutes for this activity. Ask person #5 to share with the total group their sentence. Ask for comments or questions.

4. **Point out** the paragraphs that offer information about the six research-based attributes of PLCs:
   o Fifth paragraph on shared values and beliefs
   o Sixth paragraph on shared and supported leadership development
   o Seventh paragraph on intentional collective learning
   o Eighth paragraph on structural conditions
   o Ninth paragraph on relational conditions
   o Tenth paragraph on shared personal practice

5. **Provide** each participant with "Professional Learning Communities: What Are They And Why Are They Important?" Direct their attention to pages 21–24 (the second through fifth pages of the article). Ask the participants to organize themselves into groups of six around tables. Each person then should take one of the six attributes of PLCs, read and study it, make talking points, and prepare to teach the group about his or her attribute. They can use both papers as source materials.
   Note: Divide the conditions section (structural and relational) into two parts so that there are six components for the six people to study. Provide 10–12 minutes for their study.

6. **Request** that they start teaching their group mates about their component, allowing about 2–3 minutes per person.

7. **Call** for a break, unless it has occurred earlier.

8. **After the break**, ask all the persons who taught shared values, beliefs, and visions to meet. Similarly, direct all the topics or components teachers to meet at identified points in the room. They will share what they taught their groups and prepare a strong 3-minute report to teach all their colleagues about their component, identifying a person to deliver their report.

9. **Provide closure** by having each report delivered to the whole group, with congratulations and applause given to each. The learning session leader should make concise, summary statements of relevant points about each component (see Hord & Sommers, 2008, pp. 8–16).

Future Application

Review this information in your next PLC meeting and discuss how the information might be used by the school to contribute to their development as a PLC.

Please note: The focus of the remainder of this book is how to develop each of the components.

IMAGINE

Shirley M. Hord

Scholar Emerita

Southwest Educational Development Laboratory

Imagine . . .

All professionals—teachers, administrators, counselors, media specialists/librarians—in all schools (grades K–5, 6–8, 9–12) engaged in continuous professional learning. In the professions, such as medicine and law, the membership is expected to review the journals of their field and to attend conferences. They observe each other at their work, offering feedback that leads to increased professional effectiveness. They are expected to examine and explore new methods and approaches to their work as well. Professionals, according to Webster, are characterized by a codified knowledge base, which can be increased consistently through ongoing research that seeks new means by which to expand the effectiveness of its members—and professionals maintain familiarity with the research.

Such study of one's profession, especially when done in community with others, where the learning is richer and deeper, has not been the norm of the education community. Educators have typically been isolated physically from others because of the structure of school facilities and the schedules that dominate the school day. This has resulted also in mental isolation, with no colleagues for interaction. However, knowledge is most fruitfully constructed in a social context. Providing the opportunities, the structures and schedules, for school-based educators to come together to learn in community is an important challenge.

Schools of the future will have understood that the most significant factors that determine whether students learn well are the *competence, caring, and commitment* of teachers and administrators. Their expertise, combined with their capacity for communicating and interacting meaningfully with students on their cognitive, intellectual, and emotional levels, results in powerful connections with students that enable them to learn at higher standards of quality and deeper layers of understanding. These educators have a deep commitment to their professionalism and a profound clarity about the purpose of their work. Schools of the future will have moved to support their educators in continuous study, reflection, dialogue, and learning.

They will have moved beyond arranging, solely, for elementary school grade level teams or secondary school department meetings. While teachers may well learn from their team members, their learning is restricted to the pooled knowledge and skills of their small group. Schools where educators are continuously learning make it possible for the entire faculty to convene to learn with and from each other regularly and frequently, where they introduce new sources or avenues for their study and learning. Such a structure enables the school to move uniformly toward its goals for students.

Professionals in the schools of the future will have shared and have come to clear consensus about their values and beliefs about what the school should do and what its purpose should be, as a place for learning—learning for all students and all adults. Based on their values, they will have studied the literature to determine what their school should look like and have developed a shared vision of how its educators will operate and how they will relate to each other and to students.

The positional leaders of the staff will share power and authority with the school organization's members. Members contribute to decision making, examining and studying issues in order to be sure that decisions are sound and in the best interests of their students. Further, leadership development is supported so that the school's leadership becomes distributed and is inclusive of all. This occurs as the staff members study and learn ways in which they can participate in leading the school. Such shared and supported leadership development increases teachers' assessment of their value and contributes to their professionalism.

Intentional collective learning is the hallmark of the school staff. This learning can occur in small grade level teams in the elementary school and in departments in secondary schools. But, because these teams have typically met to care for management issues, they will require the development of skills to access relevant research and resources for their learning. Importantly, so that all professionals stay on course with the school's focus and goals, regularly and frequently the entire staff comes together for learning in community. Thus, learning how to learn together is a skill to be developed.

In these schools, conditions will be present that support the community of professionals in their learning. These conditions take two forms: the structural or physical, and the human or relational conditions. As noted, one of the challenges in making learning in community possible for the professionals in the school is the arrangement of time and schedules so that the staff can come together for this important work. Resources, both human and material, contribute to the success of the adult learning community. District and state policies, as well as the parent and business community's understanding about the continuous learning needs of the staff, will be influential. These and other factors contribute to the structural conditions that support the learning of the adults.

Relational conditions are also vital to the success and effective functioning of the professionals' community of learners. Trust is a prime factor in the development of positive and productive relationships of the staff, and building trust is given attention and effort. All members of the community develop trust in their colleagues and become trustworthy so that open dialogue, discussion, and debate can occur. This suggests that conflict resolution has been addressed and an approach agreeable to all is in place.

Undoubtedly, the most demanding relationships are those that support teachers in requesting other teachers to visit them in their classrooms, observe the host teacher at work, with feedback provided by the visiting teacher. This feature of the professional learning community is likely the last to develop as it requires abundant trust and openness to critique. This peer-to-peer observing, critiquing, and learning contributes not only to the effectiveness of the individual teacher, and administrator, but to the school organization as well.

Imagine . . . educators in the future have become true professionals through their work as a professional learning community—working, just as the three words connote: *professionals* coming together in *community* to continuously *learn*, in order to increase their effectiveness so that students become increasingly successful learners.

PROFESSIONAL LEARNING COMMUNITIES: WHAT ARE THEY AND WHY ARE THEY IMPORTANT?

Shirley M. Hord

Introduction

In education circles, the term learning community has become commonplace. It is being used to mean any number of things, such as extending classroom practice into the community; bringing community personnel into the school to enhance the curriculum and learning tasks for students; or engaging students, teachers, and administrators simultaneously in learning—to suggest just a few.

This paper focuses on what Astuto, Clark, Read, McGree, and Fernandez (1993) label the professional community of learners, in which the teachers in a school and its administrators continuously seek and share learning and then act on what they learn. The goal of their actions is to enhance their effectiveness as professionals so that students benefit. This arrangement has also been termed communities of continuous inquiry and improvement.

As an organizational arrangement, the professional learning community is seen as a powerful staff development approach and a potent strategy for school change and improvement. Thus, persons at all levels of the educational system concerned about school improvement—state department personnel, intermediate service agency staff, district and campus administrators, teacher leaders, key parents and local school community members—should find this paper of interest.

This paper represents an abbreviation of Hord's review of the literature (1997), which explored the concept and operationalization of professional learning communities and their outcomes for staff and students.

The Beginnings of Professional Learning Community

During the eighties, Rosenholtz (1989) brought teachers' workplace factors into the discussion of teaching quality, maintaining that teachers who felt supported in their own ongoing learning and classroom practice were more committed and effective than those who did not receive such confirmation. Support by means of teacher networks, cooperation among colleagues, and expanded professional roles increased teacher efficacy in meeting students' needs. Further, Rosenholtz found that teachers with a high sense of their own efficacy were more likely to adopt new classroom behaviors and also more likely to stay in the profession.

McLaughlin and Talbert (1993) confirmed Rosenholtz's findings, suggesting that when teachers had opportunities for collaborative inquiry and the learning related to it, they were able to develop and share a body of wisdom gleaned from their experience. Adding to the discussion, Darling-Hammond (1996) cited shared decision making as a factor in curriculum reform and the transformation of teaching roles in some schools. In such schools, structured time is provided for teachers to work together in planning instruction, observing each other's classrooms, and sharing feedback. These and other attributes characterize professional learning communities.

Attributes of Professional Learning Communities

The literature on professional learning communities repeatedly gives attention to five attributes of such organizational arrangements:

1. supportive and shared leadership,

2. intentional collective learning,

3. shared values and vision,

4. supportive conditions, and

5. shared personal practice.

Each of these is discussed briefly in this paper.

Supportive and Shared Leadership

The school change and educational leadership literatures clearly recognize the role and influence of the campus administrator (principal, and sometimes assistant principal) on whether change will occur in the school. It seems clear that transforming a school organization into a learning community can be done only with the sanction of the leaders and the active nurturing of the entire staff's development as a community. Thus, a look at the principal of a school whose staff is a professional learning community seems a good starting point for describing what these learning communities look like and how the principal "accepts a collegial relationship with teachers" (D. Rainey, personal communication, March 13, 1997) to share leadership, power, and decision making.

Lucianne Carmichael, the first resident principal of the Harvard University Principal Center and a principal who nurtured a professional community of learners in her own school, discusses the position of authority and power typically held by principals, in which the staff views them as all-wise and all-competent (1982). Principals have internalized this "omnicompetence," Carmichael asserts. Others in the school reinforce it, making it difficult for principals to admit that they themselves can benefit from professional development opportunities, or to recognize the dynamic potential of staff contributions to decision making. Furthermore, when the principal's position is so thoroughly dominant, it is difficult for staff to propose divergent views or ideas about the school's effectiveness.

Carmichael proposes that the notion of principals' omnicompetence be "ditched" in favor of their participation in their own professional development. Kleine-Kracht (1993) concurs and suggests that administrators, along with teachers, must be learners too, "questioning, investigating, and seeking solutions" (p. 393) for school improvement. The traditional pattern that "teachers teach, students learn, and administrators manage is completely altered . . . [There is] no longer a hierarchy of who knows more than someone else, but rather the need for everyone to contribute" (p. 393).

This new relationship forged between administrators and teachers leads to shared and collegial leadership in the school, where all grow professionally and learn to view themselves (to use an athletic metaphor) as "all playing on the same team and working toward the same goal: a better school" (Hoerr, 1996, p. 381).

Louis and Kruse (1995) identify the supportive leadership of principals as one of the necessary human resources for restructuring staff into school-based professional communities. The authors refer to these principals as "post-heroic leaders who do not view themselves as the architects of school effectiveness" (p. 234). Prestine (in O'Neil, 1995) also defines characteristics of principals in schools that undertake school restructuring: a willingness to share authority, the capacity to facilitate the work of staff, and the ability to participate without dominating.

Sergiovanni (1994b) explains that "the sources of authority for leadership are embedded in shared ideas" (p. 214), not in the power of position. Snyder, Acker-Hocevar, and Snyder (1996) assert that it is also important that the principal believe that teachers have the capacity to respond to the needs of students, that this belief "provides moral strength for principals to meet difficult political and educational challenges along the way" (p. 19). Senge (quoted by O'Neil, 1995) adds that the principal's job is to create an environment in which the staff can learn continuously; "[t]hen in turn, . . . the job of the superintendent is to find principals and support [such] principals" (p. 21) who create this environment.

An additional dimension, then, is a chief executive of the school district who supports and encourages continuous learning of its professionals. This observation suggests that no longer can leaders be thought of as top-down agents of change or seen as the visionaries of the corporation; instead leaders must be regarded as democratic teachers.

Intentional Collective Learning

In 1990, Peter Senge's book *The Fifth Discipline* arrived in bookstores and began popping up in the boardrooms of corporate America. Over the next year or so, the book and its description of learning organizations, which might serve to increase organizational capacity and creativity, moved into the educational environment. The idea of a learning organization "where people continually expand their capacity to create the results they truly desire, where new and expansive patterns of thinking are nurtured, where collective aspiration is set free, and where people are continually learning how to learn together" (p. 3) caught the attention of educators who were struggling to plan and implement reform in the nation's schools. As Senge's paradigm shift was explored by educators and shared in educational journals, the label became learning communities.

In schools, the learning community is demonstrated by people from multiple constituencies, at all levels, collaboratively and continually working together (Louis & Kruse, 1995). Such collaborative work is grounded in what Newmann (reported by Brandt, 1995) and Louis and Kruse label reflective dialogue, in which staff conduct conversations about students and teaching and learning, identifying related issues and problems. Griffin (cited by Sergiovanni, 1994a, p. 154) refers to these activities as inquiry and believes that as principals and teachers inquire together they create community. Inquiry helps them to overcome chasms caused by various specializations of grade level and subject matter. Inquiry forces debate among teachers about what is important. Inquiry promotes understanding and appreciation for the work of others. . . . And inquiry helps principals and teachers create the ties that bond them together as a special group and that bind them to a shared set of ideas. Inquiry, in other words, helps principals and teachers become a community of learners.

Participants in such conversations learn to apply new ideas and information to problem solving and therefore are able to create new conditions for students. Key tools in this process are shared values and vision; supportive physical, temporal, and social conditions; and a shared personal practice. We will look at each of these in turn.

Shared Values and Vision

"Vision is a trite term these days, and at various times it refers to mission, purpose, goals, objectives, or a sheet of paper posted near the principal's office" (Isaacson & Bamburg, 1992, p. 42). Sharing vision is not just agreeing with a good idea; it is a particular mental image of what is important to an individual and to an organization. Staff are encouraged not only to be involved in the process of developing a shared vision but to use that vision as a guidepost in making decisions about teaching and learning in the school (ibid.).

A core characteristic of the vision is an undeviating focus on student learning, maintains Louis and Kruse (1995), in which each student's potential achievement is carefully considered. These shared values and vision lead to binding norms of behavior that the staff supports.

In such a community, the individual staff member is responsible for his/her actions, but the common good is placed on a par with personal ambition. The relationships between individuals are described as caring. Such caring is supported by open communication, made possible by trust (Fawcett, 1996).

Supportive Conditions

Several kinds of factors determine when, where, and how the staff can regularly come together as a unit to do the learning, decision making, problem solving, and creative work that characterize a professional learning community. In order for learning communities to function productively, the physical or structural conditions and the human qualities and capacities of the people involved must be optimal (Boyd, 1992; Louis & Kruse, 1995).

Physical conditions. Louis and Kruse (1995) identify the following physical factors that support learning communities: time to meet and talk, small school size and physical proximity of the staff to one another, interdependent teaching roles, well-developed communication structures, school autonomy, and teacher empowerment. An additional factor is the staff's input in selecting teachers and administrators for the school, and even encouraging staff who are not in tune with the program to find work elsewhere.

Boyd (1992) presents a similar list of physical factors that result in an environment conducive to school change and improvement: the availability of resources; schedules and structures that reduce isolation; policies that encourage greater autonomy, foster collaboration, enhance effective communication, and provide for staff development. Time is clearly a resource: "Time, or more properly lack of it, is one of the most difficult problems faced by schools and districts." (Watts & Castle, 1993, p. 306). Time is a significant issue for faculties who wish to work together collegially, and it has been cited as both a barrier (when it is not available) and a supportive factor (when it is available) by staffs engaging in school improvement.

People capacities. One of the first characteristics cited by Louis and Kruse (1995) of individuals in a productive learning community is a willingness to accept feedback and to work toward improvement. In addition, the following qualities are needed: respect and trust among colleagues at the school and district level, possession of an appropriate cognitive and skill base that enables effective teaching and learning, supportive leadership from administrators and others in key roles, and relatively intensive socialization processes.

Note the strong parallel with the people or human factors identified by Boyd (1992): positive teacher attitudes toward schooling, students, and change; students' heightened interest and engagement with learning (which could be construed as both an outcome and an input, it seems); norms of continuous critical inquiry and continuous improvement; a widely shared vision or sense of purpose; a norm of involvement in decision making; collegial relationships among teachers; positive, caring student-teacher-administrator relationships; a sense of community in the school; and two factors beyond the school staff—supportive community attitudes and parents and community members as partners and allies.

Boyd (1992) points out that the physical and people factors are highly interactive, many of them influencing the others. Boyd and Hord (1994) clustered the factors into four overarching functions that help build a context conducive to change and improvement: reducing staff isolation, increasing staff capacity, providing a caring and productive environment, and improving the quality of the school's programs for students.

Shared Personal Practice

Review of a teacher's behavior by colleagues is the norm in the professional learning community (Louis & Kruse, 1995). This practice is not evaluative but is part of the "peers helping peers" process. Such review is conducted regularly by teachers, who visit each other's classrooms to observe, script notes, and discuss their observations with the visited peer. The process is based on the desire for individual and community improvement and is enabled by the mutual respect and trustworthiness of staff members.

Wignall (1992) describes a high school in which teachers share their practice and enjoy a high level of collaboration in their daily work life. Mutual respect and understanding are the fundamental requirements for this kind of workplace culture. Teachers find help, support, and trust as a result of developing warm relationships with each other. "Teachers tolerate (even encourage) debate, discussion and disagreement. They are comfortable sharing both their successes and their failures. They praise and recognize one another's triumphs, and offer empathy and support for each other's troubles" (p. 18). One of the conditions that supports such a culture is the involvement of the teachers in interviewing, selecting, and hiring new teachers. They feel a commitment to their selections and to ensuring the effectiveness of the entire staff.

One goal of reform is to provide appropriate learning environments for students. Teachers, too, need "an environment that values and supports hard work, the acceptance of challenging tasks, risk taking, and the promotion of growth" (Midgley & Wood, 1993, p. 252). Sharing their personal practice contributes to creating such a setting.

Summary of Attributes

Reports in the literature are quite clear about what successful professional learning communities look like and act like. The requirements necessary for such organizational arrangements include the following:

- The collegial and facilitative participation of the principal, who shares leadership—and thus power and authority—through inviting staff input in decision making
- A shared vision that is developed from staff's unswerving commitment to students' learning and that is consistently articulated and referenced for the staff's work
- Collective learning among staff and application of that deliberate learning to solutions that address students' needs
- The visitation and review of each teacher's classroom behavior by peers as a feedback and assistance activity to support individual and community improvement
- Physical conditions and human capacities that support such an operation

Outcomes of Professional Learning Communities for Staff and Students

What difference does it make if staff are communally organized? What results, if any, might be gained from this kind of arrangement? An abbreviated report of staff and student outcomes in schools where staff are engaged together in professional learning communities follows. This report comes from the summary of results included in the literature review noted above (Hord, 1997, p. 27).

For staff, the following results have been observed:

- Reduction of isolation of teachers
- Increased commitment to the mission and goals of the school and increased vigor in working to strengthen the mission

- Shared responsibility for the total development of students and collective responsibility for students' success
- Powerful learning that defines good teaching and classroom practice and that creates new knowledge and beliefs about teaching and learners
- Increased meaning and understanding of the content that teachers teach and the roles they play in helping all students achieve expectations
- Higher likelihood that teachers will be well informed, professionally renewed, and inspired to inspire students
- More satisfaction, higher morale, and lower rates of absenteeism
- Significant advances in adapting teaching to the students, accomplished more quickly than in traditional schools
- Commitment to making significant and lasting changes
- Higher likelihood of undertaking fundamental systemic change (p. 27)

For students, the results include the following:

- Decreased dropout rate and fewer classes "skipped"
- Lower rates of absenteeism
- Increased learning that is distributed more equitably in the smaller high schools
- Greater academic gains in math, science, history, and reading than in traditional schools
- Smaller achievement gaps between students from different backgrounds (p. 28)

For more information about these important professional learning community outcomes, please refer to the literature review (Hord, 1997).

In Conclusion

If strong results such as the above are linked to teachers and administrators working in professional learning communities, how might the frequency of such communities in schools be increased? A paradigm shift is needed both by the public and by teachers themselves, about what the role of teacher entails. Many in the public and in the profession believe that the only legitimate use of teachers' time is standing in front of the class, working directly with students. In studies comparing how teachers around the globe spend their time, it is clear that in countries such as Japan, teachers teach fewer classes and use a greater portion of their time to plan, confer with colleagues, work with students individually, visit other classrooms, and engage in other professional development activities (Darling-Hammond, 1994, 1996). Bringing about changes in perspective that will enable the public and the profession to understand and value teachers' professional development will require focused and concerted effort. As Lucianne Carmichael has said, "Teachers are the first learners." Through their participation in a professional learning community, teachers become more effective, and student outcomes increase—a goal upon which we can all agree.

References

Astuto, T. A., Clark, D. L., Read, A. M., McGree, K. & Fernandez, L. de K. P. (1993). *Challenges to dominant assumptions controlling educational reform.* Andover, Massachusetts: Regional Laboratory for the Educational Improvement of the Northeast and Islands.

Boyd, V. (1992). *School context. Bridge or barrier to change?* Austin, Texas: Southwest Educational Development Laboratory.

Boyd, V., & Hord, S. M. (1994). *Principals and the new paradigm: Schools as learning communities.* Paper presented at the annual meeting of the American Educational Research Association, New Orleans.

Brandt, R. (1995, November). *On restructuring schools: A conversation with Fred Newmann*. Educational Leadership, 53(3), 70-73.

Carmichael, L. (1982, October). Leaders as learners: A possible dream. *Educational Leadership, 40*(1), 58-59.

Darling-Hammond, L. (1994, November). *The current status of teaching and teacher development in the United States*. New York: Teachers College, Columbia University.

Darling-Hammond, L. (1996, March). The quiet revolution: Rethinking teacher development. *Educational Leadership, 53*(6), 4-10.

Fawcett, G. (1996, Winter). Moving another big desk. *Journal of Staff Development, 17*(1), 34-36.

Hoerr, T. R. (1996, January). Collegiality: A new way to define instructional leadership. *Phi Delta Kappan*, 77(5), 380-381.

Hord, S. M. (1997). *Professional learning communities: Communities of continuous inquiry and improvement*. Austin: Southwest Educational Development Laboratory.

Isaacson, N., & Bamburg, J. (1992, November). Can schools become learning organizations? *Educational Leadership, 50*(3), 42-44.

Kleine-Kracht, P. A. (1993, July). The principal in a community of learning. *Journal of School Leadership*, 3(4), 391-399.

Louis, K. S., & Kruse, S. D. (1995). *Professionalism and community: Perspectives on reforming urban schools*. Thousand Oaks, California: Corwin.

McLaughlin, M. W., & Talbert, J. E. (1993). *Contexts that matter for teaching and learning*. Stanford, California: Center for Research on the Context of Secondary School Teaching, Stanford University.

Midgley, C., & Wood, S. (1993, November). Beyond site-based management: Empowering teachers to reform schools. *Phi Delta Kappan, 75*(3), 245-252.

O'Neil, J. (2005, April). On schools as learning organizations: A conversation with Peter Senge. *Educational Leadership, 52*(7), 20–23.

Prestine, N. A. (1993, July). In O'Neil, J. (1993). Extending the essential schools metaphor: Principal as enabler. *Journal of School Leadership, 3*(4), 356–379.

Rosenholtz, S. (1989). *Teacher's workplace: The social organization of schools*. New York: Longman.

Senge, P. (1990). *The fifth discipline: The art and practice of the learning organization*. New York: Currency Doubleday.

Sergiovanni, T. J. (1994a). *Building community in schools*. San Francisco: Jossey-Bass.

Sergiovanni, T. J. (1994b, May). Organizations or communities? Changing the metaphor changes the theory. *Educational Administration Quarterly, 30*(2), 214-226.

Sergiovanni, T. J. (1996). *Leadership for the schoolhouse*. San Francisco: Jossey-Bass.

Snyder, K. J., Acker-Hocevar, M., & Snyder, K. M. (1996, Winter). Principals speak out on changing school work cultures. *Journal of Staff Development, 17*(1), 14-19.

Spears, J. D., & Oliver, J. P. (1996). *Rural school reform: Creating a community of learners*. Paper presented at the annual meeting of the American Education Research Association, New York City.

Sykes, G. (1996, March). Reform of and as professional development. *Phi Delta Kappan, 77*(7), 465-476.

Watts, G. D., & Castle, S. (1993, December). The time dilemma in school restructuring. *Phi Delta Kappan, 75*(3), 306-310.

Whyte, D. (1994). The heart aroused: Poetry and the preservation of the soul in corporate America. New York: Currency Doubleday.

Wignall, R. (1992, June). *Building a collaborative school culture: A case study of one woman in the principalship*. Paper presented at the European Conference on Educational Research, Enschede, The Netherlands.

Credits and Disclaimers

Reproduced with permission of SEDL. Hord, S. M., (1997, Revised). Professional Learning Communities: What are they and why are they important? *Issues . . .* http://www.sedl.org/change/issues/issues61.html. Austin, TX: Southwest Educational Development Laboratory. *Source: Issues . . . about Change*, Vol. 6, No. 1 (1997).

Issues . . . about Change is published and produced quarterly by Southwest Educational Development Laboratory (SEDL). This publication is based on work sponsored by the Office of Educational Research & Improvement, U.S. Department of Education under grant number RJ96006801. The content herein does not necessarily reflect the views of the department or any other agency of the U.S. government or any other source. Available in alternative formats.

Component 1

Shared Beliefs, Values, and Vision

OVERVIEW AND CURRENT THINKING

Shared beliefs are the foundation for the shared values staff members hold for the school. The vision for the school—how it operates and the purpose for which it exists—is consequently grounded in these values. A collaborative process should be employed by the administrators and teachers to develop and articulate their shared vision.

In schools where administrators and teachers learn and work together as a PLC, the focus is unceasingly on students and their successful learning. The staff members' commitment to their own continuous learning is directed by evidence of students' learning. This efficacious staff believes that each student has the capacity to learn well. The staff creates the vision and, subsequently, the environment wherein all students will reach their potential. The vision is kept visible and is revisited often to ensure its currency and authenticity.

Although each member of the learning community is responsible for his or her own behaviors, the common good is given priority for action. The relationships of the individuals are supported by their caring about each other, trust in each other, open communication with each other, and by their belief that they can consistently increase their competence through their shared learning. The community members all strive toward a vision of enhanced quality teaching so that all students will be successful learners who meet high standards.

LEARNING OPPORTUNITY 1.1

My Personal Learning Compass

Learning is the making of meaning.

—Robert Kegan

Outcome

PLC members will identify and understand their unique approach to learning.

Assumption

Learning within a group can often create conflicts or confusion because of different approaches to learning. The better we understand our own personal orientation as a learner, the more likely it is that we will be able to accept how others learn in ways different from our own ways.

Suggested Time

45–60 minutes

Materials

- Colored dots
- "Navigating Learning" (see p. 31; one copy for each participant)
- "Personal Learning Compass" (see p. 33; one copy for each participant)

Learning Event

1. **Set the stage** by asking PLC members to describe a time when they found learning fun and interesting, and a time they found learning difficult and boring. Ask them what might have been happening for learning to have been experienced in two different ways. After having PLC members share their stories, invite them to find a partner for the remainder of this activity.

2. **Give** each member a copy of "Navigating Learning" and of the "Personal Learning Compass." Inform members this activity will help each of them to identify a possible preferred approach in how they like to learn.

3. **Invite** members to read "Navigating Learning" and then turn to their partners to discuss what might be important in thinking about learning across two poles: perceiving and processing. Depending on time, you might gather some of their key insights on flip-chart paper.

4. **Direct** PLC members to "Personal Learning Compass." Give each person two sticky dots and ask him or her to locate the large square with a target in the middle.

   Ask each person to place one dot on the vertical line (*preferred perceptual learning*) that feels most like him or her, and one dot on the horizontal line (*preferred process for learning*) that feels most like him or her. The vertical and horizontal poles are identified as 1 (less like me) and 4 (most like me).

5. **Develop** a "Personal Learning Compass" for the whole PLC. When everyone has finished, ask any member who had a dot in the *Perceive Concretely* section to raise his or her hand. Count the raised hands and put the number in that section. Do this for the other three orientations: *Perceive Abstractly*, *Reflective Processing*, *Active Processing*. After you have charted the learning preferences for the PLC members, ask them to predict what might be their strengths in working together and what might be some challenges.

6. **Ask** members to take about 5 minutes and write a story (on the back of the paper) of a time they experienced learning at its best. When they have completed their stories, ask the members to scan the story they wrote and look for clues about their preferred way of learning. They should then check as many boxes that feel appropriate in the upper left corner of the "Personal Learning Compass," *I prefer to learn . . .*

7. **Bring closure** by asking members to think about orientations that are opposite from their own and to consider what behaviors they could express that would support a

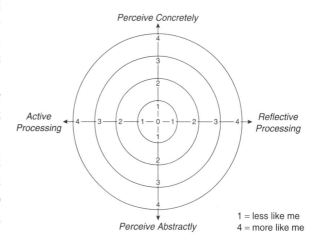

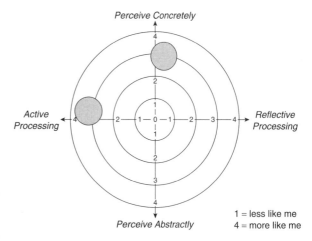

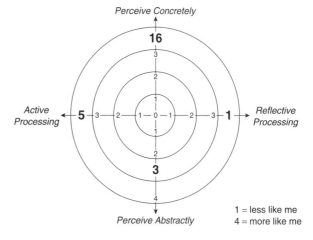

different type of learner. For example, a person who rates high in preferring to experience learning concretely might accommodate a different learning style by expressing patience when members want to discuss ideas in detail.

8. Finally, **invite** members to write in the box in the lower-left-hand corner what behaviors they could express for each learner who learns differently from the way they learn.

Future Application

Take the "Personal Learning Compass" for the whole group and enlarge it so it can be clearly visible where you meet. You can use it for a checkout at the end of a meeting to make sure all learning orientations are being supported and acknowledged. You might also reference it if conflict arises in the PLC. Often conflict can occur because different learning orientations are not being considered or supported in the PLC.

Notes:

Navigating Learning

James L. Roussin

Each of us has a preferred way of perceiving and processing experiences—of interacting with our world. We call this a learning style. A learning style is a description of consistent preferences each of us has for the way we like to receive, process, and package information.

—McCarthy & O'Neill-Blackwell (2007)

When navigating across unknown or unfamiliar terrain, it is helpful to have a compass. A compass can give us a sense of comfort and direction, even when our surroundings are not familiar. Sometimes when working with others in the PLC we can feel lost or confused. When that happens, it can be helpful to have a compass to guide us through the different ways each person experiences and expresses his or her own learning.

The "Personal Learning Compass" (see p. 33) identifies and charts the learning preferences of PLC members across two dimensions. The *vertical dimension* engages learning on a *perceptual* level. The *horizontal dimension* engages learning on a processing level. These two dimensions operate together to frame a learning preference for a group or an individual. Kurt Lewin (1951) was the first to identify these two dimensions. Lewin was a psychologist who developed the basis for much of today's basic learning theory.

The Vertical Dimension

The vertical dimension of learning moves between two *perceptual* poles: the concrete and the abstract. Donald Kolb referenced the *concrete* as our *immediate experience* that is embraced in deep feeling tones (sensate). When a learner is oriented toward the concrete, he or she likes sensory-based learning and personal involvement. The learner enjoys interacting with others through personal discovery. When a learner prefers the *abstract* pole, he or she likes to engage thinking through logic and theory in order to conceptualize for understanding. At this end of the pole the learner prefers to have his or her thinking mediated through new ideas or concepts.

Bernice McCarthy suggested, "The tension between these two ways of perceiving is the central dynamic in learning" (McCarthy, 2000, p. 27). We like to think of the two perceptual poles as polarities. They are like breathing. If you only inhale and never exhale, you will quickly run into problems. The greatest potential for learning occurs when a person or team is flexible enough to engage perceptual learning at each end of the two poles.

The Horizontal Dimension

The horizontal dimension of learning moves between two *processing* poles: active and reflective. When the learner prefers the *reflective* processing pole, he or she likes to rely on *thoughts and feelings* to create new knowledge. From this position the learner is in an observer role, watching or developing insight about his or her own experiences.

In the *active* processing pole, the learner prefers *active experimentation*, like constructing, building, or writing. The learner also prefers a practical approach on topics that are relevant and immediate. *Active* learners tend to retain and understand information best by doing something active with it.

It is helpful to remember that when facilitating the learning in a PLC each person has his or her own preference for learning. That preference is guided by an internal compass. If PLC members are not aware of the different approaches to learning, they may be less patient in dealing with others who have an orientation to learning that is different from their own. The "Personal Learning Compass" on page 33 can help the PLC identify and map out different learning approaches across two critical dimensions, perceiving and processing.

Notes:

A learning story: write about a time when you experienced learning at its *best!*

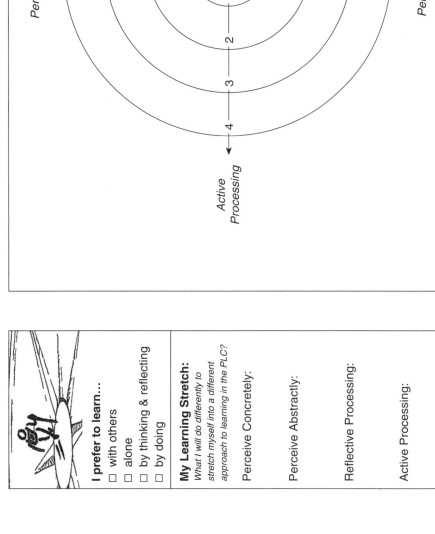

I prefer to learn...
- ☐ with others
- ☐ alone
- ☐ by thinking & reflecting
- ☐ by doing

My Learning Stretch:
What I will do differently to stretch myself into a different approach to learning in the PLC?

Perceive Concretely:

Perceive Abstractly:

Reflective Processing:

Active Processing:

Reflective Processing

Perceive Concretely

Active Processing

Perceive Abstractly

1 = less like me
4 = more like me

Source: Concept by David A. Kolb. (1984). Adaptation and design by James L. Roussin.

LEARNING OPPORTUNITY 1.2

Creating a Culture of Academic Optimism

Mastery or enactive experiences are the most powerful source of efficacy information. The perception that a performance has been successful raises efficacy beliefs, which contributes to the expectation of proficient performance in the future.

—Goddard, Hoy, & Woolfolk Hoy (2004)

Outcome

This learning opportunity identifies critical research around the importance of building collective efficacy and academic optimism within the PLC.

> **Academic optimism.** The belief staff members carry about the control they have in making a difference for student learning. When there is high academic optimism, the faculty believes they can make a difference in helping every student learn and be successful.

Assumption

When PLC members hold high academic optimism for making a difference in student learning and see the results of their efforts, they nurture collective efficacy. Collective efficacy in return builds hope and courage to take on the most difficult challenges facing schools today.

Suggested Time

60–90 minutes

Materials

- Flip chart and markers
- Research Briefs 1–4 (see pp. 36, 37, 39, and 41; one set for each participant)
- "Creating a Culture of Academic Optimism" (see p. 43; one copy for each participant)

Learning Event

1. **Set the stage** by asking the members in the PLC to identify the critical factors that make the greatest difference in improving schools for student learning. As members are reporting out, chart the ideas on a flip chart. After everyone has reported out, inform the group members they are going to read some of the most pertinent research to date

for improving schools. They should be on the lookout for where their ideas connect to the research, and for where they don't.

2. **Share** the four research briefs. First, have PLC members count off up to the number four. Give each participant the research brief corresponding to his or her number. The group members should take 10–15 minutes to read and highlight key ideas from the briefs. After each person has had enough time to read, he or she should join others who read the same brief and discuss with them important learning that would benefit the whole group. One person should write on a flip chart the concepts the group thinks are important to everyone. This can take from 10 to 20 minutes, depending on the group. At the end of the charting, have each small group report to the larger group what they feel is important.

3. After everyone has reported out, **ask** each group to add one more sheet of flip-chart paper next to the key learning. On the flip-chart paper, have them create a T-chart. On the left side, write the heading, What We Are Already Doing! On the right side, write the heading, What Else Might We Do?

4. **Invite** each group to start filling out the chart. Once that is complete, have groups move from chart to chart and identify what is already in place in the school and what might be put in place in the future.

5. **Provide closure** by handing out copies of "Creating a Culture of Academic Optimism" and requesting each group to identify possible next steps to embed more intentionally their research concept in the work of the PLC during the next 2 months. Each small group might also create two or three action steps the PLC can take to implement the research into practice.

Future Application

The PLC should consider creating a yearly action plan based on the research of academic optimism. Once the action plan is developed, determine a way to evaluate progress and determine how this effort is making a difference for students and their learning.

Notes:

RESEARCH BRIEF 1

Academic Emphasis of Schools (Group 1)

Academic emphasis is the extent to which the school is driven by a *quest* for academic excellence—a press for academic achievement. High but achievable academic goals are set for students, the learning environment is orderly and serious, students are motivated to work hard, and students respect academic achievement (Hoy & Miskel, 2005; Hoy, Tarter, & Kottkamp, 1991).

Hoy and his colleagues (1991) were first to demonstrate that the collective property academic emphasis of the school was positively and directly related to student achievement in high schools while controlling for SES (socioeconomic status). Whether school effectiveness was conceived as the commitment of teachers to the school, the teachers' judgment of the effectiveness of the school, or actual student test scores, academic emphasis remained a potent force. At both middle school and high school, academic emphasis and achievement were positively related, even after controlling for socioeconomic factors (Hoy, Tarter, & Bliss, 1990; Hoy & Hannum, 1997; Hoy and Sabo, 1998).

The findings are the same for elementary schools. Goddard, Sweetland, and Hoy (2000), controlling for SES, school size, student race, and gender, used hierarchical linear modeling to find academic emphasis an important element in explaining achievement in both math and reading. The authors concluded, "Elementary schools with strong academic emphases positively affect achievement for poor and minority students" (p. 698).

Alig-Mielcarek and Hoy (2005) considered the influence of the instructional leadership of the principal and the academic press of the school. They also found that academic emphasis was significant in explaining student achievement, even controlling for SES. They found that academic emphasis of the school, not instructional leadership, was the critical variable explaining achievement. In fact, instructional leadership worked indirectly, not directly, through academic press to influence student achievement.

The results are consistent, whether the level was elementary, middle, or secondary: academic emphasis is a key variable in explaining student achievement, even controlling for socioeconomic status, previous achievement, and other demographic variables.

Academic Emphasis

The one goal that virtually everyone shares for schools is academic achievement of students. The reform and accountability movements have promoted a press toward the academic achievement of all students (No Child Left Behind). The focus of schooling is clear: it is academic. A push for academic achievement, however, in an environment where teachers do not feel efficacious, is a recipe for frustration and stress. The challenge is to create school conditions in which teachers believe they and their students are up to the task. How might this be done? Principals move a school by example. They celebrate the achievements of students and faculty, especially the academic ones. An emphasis on the honor roll, national honor societies, and exemplary student work of all kinds are examples of behaviors that foster academics. To be sure, this is an old list, but in conjunction with building efficacy and trust, these activities take on new strength.

From Hoy, W. K., Tarter, C. J., & Woolfolk Hoy, A. (2006). Academic optimism of schools: A force for student achievement. *American Educational Research Journal, 43*, 425-446. Used with Permission.

RESEARCH BRIEF 2

Collective Efficacy (Group 2)

Social cognitive theory (Bandura, 1977, 1997) is a general framework for understanding human learning and motivation. Self-efficacy, a critical component of the theory, is an individual's belief in her or his capacity to organize and execute the actions required to produce a given level of attainment (Bandura, 1997). Efficacy beliefs are central mechanisms in human agency, the intentional pursuit of a course of action. Individuals and groups are unlikely to initiate action without a positive sense of efficacy. The strength of efficacy beliefs affects the choices individuals and schools make about their future plans and actions.

Student achievement and sense of efficacy are related. Researchers have found positive associations between student achievement and three kinds of efficacy beliefs: self-efficacy beliefs of students (Pajares, 1994, 1997), self-efficacy beliefs of teachers (Tschannen-Moran, Woolfolk Hoy, & Hoy, 1998), and teachers' collective efficacy beliefs about the school (Goddard, Hoy, & Woolfolk Hoy, 2000). We focus on collective efficacy of schools and student achievement because collective efficacy is a school property amenable to change.

Within schools, perceived collective efficacy represents the judgments of the group about the performance capability of the social system as a whole (Bandura, 1997). Teachers have efficacy beliefs about themselves as well as about the entire faculty. Simply put, perceived collective efficacy is the judgment of the teachers that the faculty as a whole can organize and execute actions required to have a positive effect on students (Goddard, Hoy, et al., 2004).

Bandura (1993) was first to show the relationship between sense of collective efficacy and academic school performance, a relationship that existed in spite of low socioeconomic status. Schools in which the faculty had a strong sense of collective efficacy flourished, whereas those in which faculty had serious doubts about their collective efficacy withered—that is, declined or showed little academic progress. Continuing research has provided support for the importance of collective efficacy in explaining student achievement. Goddard, Hoy et al. (2000) supported the role of collective efficacy in promoting school achievement in urban elementary schools. They hypothesized that perceived collective efficacy would enhance student achievement in mathematics and reading. After controlling for SES, they found that collective efficacy was significantly related to student achievement in urban elementary schools.

Hoy, Sweetland, and Smith (2002), continuing this line of inquiry and using collective efficacy as the central variable, predicted school achievement in high schools. They found collective efficacy was the key variable in explaining student achievement. They found, in fact, that it was more important than either socioeconomic status or academic press. Hoy and his colleagues (2002) concluded, "School norms that support academic achievement and collective efficacy are particularly important in motivating teachers and students to achieve . . . however, academic press is most potent when collective efficacy is strong" (p. 89). That is, academic press works through collective efficacy. They further theorized that when collective efficacy was strong, an emphasis on academic pursuits directed teacher behaviors, helped them persist, and reinforced social norms of collective efficacy.

In a similar vein, Goddard, LoGerfo, and Hoy (2004) tested a more comprehensive model of perceived collective efficacy and student achievement. They *learned* that collective efficacy explained student achievement in reading, writing, and social studies, regardless of minority student enrollment, urbanicity, SES, school size, and earlier achievement. Research has consistently demonstrated the power of positive efficacy judgments in human learning, motivation, and achievement in such diverse areas as dieting, smoking cessation, sports performance, political participation, and academic achievement (Bandura, 1997; Goddard, Hoy, et al., 2004).

Collective Efficacy

Collective efficacy is grounded in Bandura's (1997) social cognitive theory; hence, we turn to his sources of efficacy for ideas about how to build collective efficacy in schools. The sources of self-efficacy are mastery experiences, vicarious experiences, social persuasion, and affective states, each of which conveys information that influences teacher perceptions about the school (Bandura, 1993, 1997; Goddard, Hoy, et al., 2004; Pajares, 1997). For example, let's consider a school with a poor graduation rate. A neighboring district has implemented a successful program for at-risk students. The principal is in the position to orchestrate the transfer of the neighbor's success to his or her school. In so doing, the school is engaged in a self-regulatory process informed by the vicarious learning of its members and, perhaps, the social persuasion of leaders. Modeling success and persuading teachers to believe in themselves and their capabilities is a reasonable route to improve collective efficacy and enhance academic optimism (Bandura, 1997; Goddard, Hoy et al., 2004).

Notes:

From Hoy, W. K., Tarter, C. J., & Woolfolk Hoy, A. (2006). Academic optimism of schools: A force for student achievement. *American Educational Research Journal, 43,* 425-446. Used with Permission.

RESEARCH BRIEF 3

Faculty Trust in Parents and Students (Group 3)

Faculty trust in parents and students is the third school property that is related to student achievement. Faculty trust in parents and students is a collective school property in the same fashion as collective efficacy and academic emphasis. Surprisingly, trust in parents and trust in students is a unitary concept. Although one might think that the two are separate concepts, several factor analyses have demonstrated they are *not* (Hoy & Tschannen-Moran, 1999; Goddard, Tschannen-Moran, & Hoy, 2001). Furthermore, Bryk and Schneider (2002) make the theoretical argument that teacher–student trust in elementary schools operates primarily through teacher–parent trust.

Trust is one's vulnerability to another in the belief that the other will act in one's best interests. Tschannen-Moran and Hoy (2000), after an extensive review of the literature, concluded that trust is a general concept with at least five facets: benevolence, reliability, competence, honesty, and openness. Although it is theoretically possible that these facets of trust may not vary together, the research on schools shows all five facets of trust in schools do indeed vary together to form an integrated construct of faculty trust in schools, whether the schools are elementary (Hoy & Tschannen-Moran, 1999; Hoy & Tschannen-Moran, 2003) or secondary (Smith, Hoy, & Sweetland, 2001). Thus, we defined faculty trust as the group's willingness to be vulnerable to another party based on the confidence that the latter party is benevolent, reliable, competent, honest, and open (Hoy & Tschannen-Moran, 2003).

Cooperation and trust should set the stage for effective student learning, but only a few studies have examined this relationship. Goddard et al. (2001) examined the role of faculty trust in promoting school achievement of urban elementary schools. Using a multilevel model, they demonstrated a significant direct relationship between faculty trust in clients (i.e., students and parents) and higher student achievement, even controlling for socioeconomic status. Like collective efficacy, faculty trust was a key property that enabled schools to overcome some of the disadvantages of low SES.

Hoy (2002) examined the trust-achievement hypothesis in high schools and again found that faculty trust in parents and students was positively related to student achievement while controlling for SES. He theorized that trusting others is a fundamental aspect of human learning because learning is typically a cooperative process, and distrust makes cooperation virtually impossible. When students, teachers, and parents have common learning goals, then trust and cooperation are likely ingredients that improve teaching and learning.

Finally, Bryk and Schneider (2002) performed a three-year longitudinal study in 12 Chicago elementary schools. Using HLM models, survey and achievement data, and in-depth interviews, they concluded relational trust was a prime resource for school improvement. Trust and cooperation among students, teachers, and parents influenced regular student attendance, persistent learning, and faculty experimentation with new practices. In brief, trust among teachers, parents, and students produced schools that showed marked gains in student learning, whereas schools with weak trust relationships saw virtually no improvement. The research of Bryk and Schneider, and that of Hoy and his colleagues (2006a), reinforce each other in the common conclusion that faculty trust of students and parents enhances student achievement.

Trust in Parents and Students

There is some research on family and community involvement in schools (cf., Epstein, 1989). There is little systematic research on how to build authentic trust, however. Faculty trust in students and parents can be promoted through useful interchanges, both formal and informal, between parents and teachers. Making the most of vicarious learning, for example, a school can respond to a lack of trust and community participation in school activities by emulating the practices and procedures of magnet schools, which are known for their parental cooperation and involvement. But much more research is needed about what programs and factors support the development of teachers' trust in parents and students.

Such examples demonstrate how changes in social perceptions influence what actions organizations choose to pursue. Collective perceptions about efficacy, academic emphasis, and trust shape the school's normative environment and can be developed through experiences that convey their value.

Notes:

From Hoy, W. K., Tarter, C. J., & Woolfolk Hoy, A. (2006). Academic optimism of schools: A force for student achievement. *American Educational Research Journal, 43,* 425-446. Used with Permission.

RESEARCH BRIEF 4

Academic Optimism (Group 4)

Three collective properties—academic emphasis, efficacy, and trust—are not only similar in their nature and function, but also in their potent and positive influence on student achievement. The three concepts have much in common. In fact, Hoy and his colleagues (Hoy, Tarter, & Woolfolk Hoy, 2006) demonstrated that *the three collective properties worked together in a unified fashion to create a positive academic environment called academic optimism.*

Many conceptions treat optimism as a cognitive characteristic: a goal or expectancy (Peterson, 2000; Snyder et al., 2002). Our conception of academic optimism includes both cognitive and affective dimensions, and adds a behavioral element. Collective efficacy is a group belief or expectation: it is cognitive. Faculty trust in parents and teachers is an affective response. Academic emphasis is the press for particular behaviors in the school workplace (Hoy et al., 2006b). Hoy and his colleagues concluded, "Collective efficacy reflects the thoughts and beliefs of the group; faculty trust adds an affective dimension, and academic emphasis captures the behavioral enactment of efficacy and trust" (p. 14). Academic optimism is a rich picture of human agency that explains collective behavior in terms of cognitive, affective, and behavioral dimensions.

When the faculty believes it has the capability to organize and execute actions for a positive effect on student achievement, it emphasizes academic achievement, and academic emphasis in turn reinforces a strong sense of collective efficacy. In sum, all the elements of academic optimism are in transactional relationships with each other and interact to create a culture of academic optimism in the school.

Hoy & his colleagues (2006b) chose the term *academic optimism* to reflect beliefs about control in schools. They explain as follows:

> Optimism is an appropriate overarching construct to unite efficacy, trust, and academic emphasis because each concept contains a sense of the possible. Efficacy is the belief that the faculty can make a positive difference in student learning; teachers believe in themselves. Faculty trust in students and parents is the belief that teachers, parents, and students can cooperate to improve learning, that is, the faculty believes in its students. Academic emphasis is the enacted behavior prompted by these beliefs, that is, the focus is student success. Thus, a school with high academic optimism is a collectivity in which the faculty believes that it can make a difference, that students can learn, and academic performance can be achieved. (Hoy et al., 2005)

Optimism

The research on individual optimism suggests some ideas about encouraging a culture of optimism in schools. Peterson (2000) found that optimism is thwarted by stress, so decreasing stress should support optimism. Teachers can lower their stress by increasing their agency and control through appropriate participation in decisions that affect their school lives (Hoy & Tarter, 2004).

People learn from models because the observation of successful performance in others promotes an acquisition of their beliefs and the actions. The most effective models are those who seem competent, powerful, prestigious, and similar to the observer (Pintrich & Schunk, 2002).

Vicarious and observational learning are sources of optimism. *Thus teachers can serve as models for each other*. The way school problems are discussed should convey the possibilities for resolution rather defeatism. *Novice teachers, for example, should hear optimistic approaches to teaching rather than a sense of passive helplessness in teachers' lounges and school hallways.*

Our analysis is a promising clarification of the linkages within schools that influence student achievement. Although our data are drawn from high schools, we believe the findings are applicable to elementary and middle schools because the three elements of academic optimism have explained learning in those settings as well. Clearly, more research in a variety of school settings is necessary to build a comprehensive theory of academic optimism of schools.

Academic optimism is especially attractive because it emphasizes the potential of schools to overcome the power of socioeconomic factors to impair student achievement. *There is a real value in focusing on potential with its strength and resilience rather than pathology with its weakness and helplessness. Optimism attempts to explain and nurture what is best in schools to facilitate student learning.* This simple conclusion should encourage teachers and principals to move forward with confidence.

Notes:

From Hoy, W. K., Tarter, C. J., & Woolfolk Hoy, A. (2006). Academic optimism of schools: A force for student achievement. *American Educational Research Journal, 43*, 425-446. Used with Permission.

CREATING A CULTURE OF ACADEMIC OPTIMISM

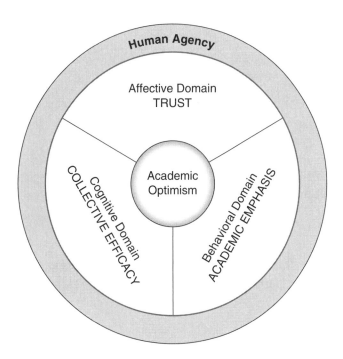

Create an action map that identifies next steps for implementing the research on academic optimism.

LEARNING OPPORTUNITY 1.3

Prioritized Abandonment

When you have disciplined people, you don't need hierarchy. When you have disciplined thought, you don't need bureaucracy.

—Collins (2001)

Outcome

This learning opportunity will help the PLC identify what might be abandoned so there is a more rigorous focus on a goal that improves student learning.

Assumption

We can easily become distracted by attending to too many things in our work, all of which can feel right and important. However, by focusing on so many things, we lose sight of what is important and may minimize our potential to make a difference.

Suggested Time

45–90 minutes

Materials

- "Prioritized Abandonment Overview" (see p. 46; one copy for each participant)
- "Prioritized Abandonment Chart" (see p. 48), enlarged so the whole group can see it
- Sticky notes (one package per participant)

Learning Event

1. **Set the stage** by asking each person in the PLC to brainstorm privately a list of personal or professional activities or actions that he or she chose to abandon at some point in the past, and to recall what occurred afterward. Have each person report out one such situation and what happened as a result.

2. **Assign** learning partners in pairs and have them read the "Prioritized Abandonment Overview." At the end of reading each paragraph, utilize the strategy of *say something.* In this strategy, there is no cross talk. Each person reads and then shares what thoughts came to mind after reading the paragraph. At the end of the reading, have each pair join another pair for a group of four and openly discuss what stands out as important after reading the text.

3. **Focus** on PLC goals with the following activity. At the end of the discussion, give each person a package of sticky notes. Have each person quietly identify one thing (on each sticky note) that they or others are doing that might be abandoned in order to focus better on the PLC goal(s). Then have the group do a silent sorting of the sticky notes by like activities. Assign a name (heading) for each activity grouping, and add the total number of notes written in each group.

4. **Show** how prioritized abandonment works by guiding the PLC to the enlarged "Prioritized Abandonment Chart." You will want the PLC to categorize each of the activities they identified on their sticky notes under one of the following headings:

   o Important and Urgent
   o Important and NOT Urgent
   o NOT Important and Urgent
   o NOT Important and NOT Urgent

   Write each heading in the appropriate area of the large chart. Check with each group to see if anything else comes to mind. After all ideas are voiced and listed on the chart, have the groups prioritize and write in the parentheses on each line of the chart the correct rank for each heading (what should be considered *first* in being abandoned, then *second* and so on).

5. **Provide closure** by having the PLC reach consensus on one or two activities that could be abandoned without harming student learning or the operation of the school or other district programs. The PLC should also determine who should be notified and included in the decision on choosing to abandon a practice, task, or initiative. Also, the PLC may need to identify what practical steps will have to be taken to actually make the abandonment happen.

Future Application

Have the PLC monitor in the weeks ahead what happens after making the decision to abandon something. You will want to check in with each other on what you are noticing and what impact, if any, is occurring based on leaving a practice, task, or initiative behind. This reporting will provide confidence for those who are unsure about the decision for choosing to abandon the practice, task, or initiative the PLC agreed on. Each successful abandonment that enhances the potential for reaching your goals prepares the PLC to be more aware of what can be abandoned in the future that is not adding value or contributing toward your most important goals.

Notes:

PRIORITIZED ABANDONMENT OVERVIEW

James L. Roussin

Never mistake motion for action.

—Ernest Hemingway

In Jim Collins's book *Good to Great,* he researched what it was that made certain organizations more successful than others. As he looked at highly successful businesses and teams, he identified "best practices" that increased the chances for reaching established goals and priorities. Collins's research led him to what he called *the Hedgehog concept.* This concept was loosely based on a Greek poem by Archilochus about a fox and a hedgehog. The poem illustrated that a fox knows many things and is easily distracted and unfocused. A hedgehog knows *one big* thing and can ignore many distractions and stay focused on what is really important. If a PLC is going to have an impact for improving student learning through the work of adult learning, then it will be important to focus collective efforts toward clear goals and not get side-tracked by the many distractions of school life.

Sometimes it is hard to distinguish a distraction from the important work. Stephen Covey in his book, *The 7 Habits of Highly Effective People* (first published in 1989), suggested that busyness in our workplaces has become the new corporate disease. Workers can often get a temporary high from solving urgent matters, which can turn into an addiction to urgency. The constant demands placed on our work today can create low levels of stress that engages the neurotransmitter epinephrine, also called adrenaline. This hormone is released when a person is confronted by environmental factors such as excitement and fear. What is important to understand from Covey's perspective is that we might be unconsciously adding unnecessary work in our jobs in order to feed our addiction to urgency. In order to break this pattern, it is important to periodically identify which things you are currently doing that you can abandon, things that are not contributing toward reaching the results of your goals or desired outcomes.

Larry Lezotte first discussed the concept of prioritized abandonment. Lezotte suggested that it was important to look carefully at current practices and stop those that were not effective or contributing toward reaching identified goals. The advantage of thoughtfully abandoning practices, tasks, and initiatives that are not contributing toward our goals is that it frees up our time so we can focus on what is important. This brings us right back to the hedgehog concept. If we want to make a meaningful difference in our PLCs, then it will be important to identify what we can abandon in order to better focus our attention and efforts on our goal(s) or desired outcomes. The prioritized abandonment chart on page 48 can help you with this process.

Commitment is what transforms a promise into reality.

It is the words that speak boldly of your intentions.

And the actions which speak louder than words.

It is making the time when there is none.

Coming through time after time, year after year.

Commitment is the stuff character is made of,

the power to change the face of things.

It is the daily triumph of integrity over skepticism.

—Author unknown

Notes:

Source: Lezotte & McKee (2002), Collins (2001), Covey (1989).

Prioritized Abandonment Chart

URGENT   **NOT URGENT**

Our Desired Outcome?

IMPORTANT

NOT IMPORTANT

LEARNING OPPORTUNITY 1.4

Discovering Our Core Values

Once people have evidence that leads them to perceive differences in values, distrust is likely to emerge.

—Sitkin & Roth (1993)

Outcome

The PLC will identify its common core values that will guide the work of learning and collaboration during the year.

Assumption

Organizations that discover the larger purpose for their work and their commitment to core values go a long way to engage human energy and passion.

Suggested Time

45–90 minutes

Materials

- 10 sheets of blank 8 1/2 x 11 paper per table
- Markers
- Masking tape
- Dots
- "Quotes" (see p. 51), photocopied and cut out so there are enough quotes to give one to each participant
- "Discovering Our Core Values" (see p. 53; one copy for each participant)

Learning Event

1. **Set the stage** by informing the PLC members that they will explore common core values for working together during the year. Give each person a quote (see "Quotes," p. 51) relating to core values, then have everyone turn to a neighbor and explain why his or her quote is important for the work of a PLC. After this, have the participants report out their understanding of what a core value is and is not. Don't move on until you are sure everyone understands the idea of a core value, especially as it relates to the workplace.

2. Ask everyone to get into a relaxed position, and, if it is comfortable for them to do so, to close their eyes. **Read** aloud the brief story "Discovering Our Core Values" at the top of

the handout. Be sure to pause frequently and read slowly so participants can visualize the images described in the story. At the end of the story, ask participants to wait quietly without talking while you give each member a copy of "Discovering Our Core Values."

3. **Facilitate** the development of common core values by asking each person to write the three messages they want to give the child. These will be written inside the boxes on the handout. Allow 5–10 minutes for everyone to write the messages. At the end of the writing, each person in the PLC will share with others in the small group what his or her core values are for the child. Ask the group to look for common themes expressed by the values everyone shares. At the end of the sharing, have someone from each small group capture the common core value themes using the markers and 8 1/2 x 11 paper. There should be one value for each sheet of paper.

4. **Build** a core values wall. Have table groups tape all the common themes on the wall. You will want to group those that are similar and have the PLC give each group a name. Give each participant three dots to identify the three core values that would be most important to guide the work of the PLC in the coming year. Ask everyone to quietly post his or her dots. After everyone has identified their most important core values, discuss where the dots were placed and why the core value with the most dots is important.

5. **Provide closure** by identifying three to four core values that will guide the PLC in the coming year. Be sure you take time and reach a consensus on the core values that have been identified as important.

Future Application

At your next PLC meeting, consider taking each core value and identifying a behavior that could be expressed by the group when doing its work. You might even start a conversation around how the core values engage the work of learning by the adults as it is connected to the learning of the students in the school. A last suggestion is to include the core values on all your PLC agendas as a reminder.

Notes:

QUOTES

Companies that illuminate the larger purpose of their work and their commitment to core values will go a long way to align and motivate all generations in their workplaces.

From *Strategies for the Intergenerational Workplace*, by K. Kirkpatrick, S. Martin, S. Warneke. Retrieved June 4, 2009, from http://www.gensler.com/uploads/documents/Inter generationalWorkplace_07_17_2008.pdf

Highly proactive people recognize their "response-ability"—the ability to choose their response. They do not blame circumstances, conditions, or conditioning for their behavior. Their behavior is a product of their own conscious choice, based on values, rather than a product of their conditions, based on feeling.

From *Daily Reflections for Highly Effective People: Living the 7 Habits of Highly Effective People Every Day* (1989) by Stephen R. Covey. New York: Fireside.

The extent to which an individual's values coincide with the shared image of her or his community determines the degree of his or her membership in that community. The level of integration that an organization will achieve during times of change will depend on the means by which it dissolves the value-conflict of its members.

From *Systems Thinking: Managing Chaos and Complexity* (2006), by J. Gharajedaghi. San Diego, CA: Butterworth-Heinemann.

A leader will find it difficult to articulate a coherent vision unless it expresses his core values, his basic identity . . . one must first embark on the formidable journey of self-discovery in order to create a vision with authentic soul.

From *Good Business: Leadership, Flow, and the Making of Meaning* (2004) by Mihaly Csikszentmihalyi. New York: Penguin.

If there are no common values, there can be no image of the future.

From *Images of the Future: The Twenty-First Century and Beyond* (1975) by Robert Bundy.

The ideals which have lighted my way, and time after time have given me new courage to face life cheerfully, have been kindness, beauty and truth.

—Albert Einstein

Values are the criteria we use to evaluate alternatives, and they allow us to set priorities. Without values, decision making would be impossible.

From *Values-Driven Change: Strategies and Tools for Long-Term Success* (2006) by Kenneth E. Hultman. Lincoln, NE: iUniverse.

Leadership is basically a matter of how to be, not how to do it. Leaders need to lead by example, with clear, consistent messages, with values that are "moral compasses," and a sense of ethics that works full time.

Frances Hesselbein, quoted in *Beat the Odds: Avoid Corporate Death and Build a Resilient Enterprise* by Robert A. Rudzki (2007). Fort Lauderdale, FL: J. Ross Publishing, Inc.

All decision-making is a values-clarifying exercise.

From *Personal Power II: The Driving Force!* (1996) by Anthony Robbins. Audio Renaissance.

Your values are a critical source of energy, enthusiasm, and direction. Work is meaningful and fun when it's an expression of your true core.

From "The Case for Optimism" (April 2005) by Shoshana Zuboff, *Fast Company (93).* Retrieved November 2008 from http://www.fastcompany.com/magazine/93/.html

DISCOVERING OUR CORE VALUES

The extent to which an individual's values coincide with the shared image of her or his community determines the degree of his or her membership in that community. The level of integration that an organization will achieve during times of change will depend on the means by which it dissolves the value conflict of its members.

—Gharajedaghi (2006)

Tell the Following Story

Imagine yourself walking down a beautiful, winding country road. It is a glorious day and the beginning of spring. As you continue your walk, you can't help but notice the deep, rich green of the budding leaves from the trees and the rolling hills of pastureland. You notice something far out ahead of you on the road. It looks like a small speck, but is traveling very fast and coming right toward you. You don't worry and continue on your walk, taking in the beauty around you. As you look down the road ahead of you, you suddenly realize that it is another human being coming right toward you and it looks like a young child. This child looks familiar and you soon realize it is *you* when you were a child. You get to give this child three important life messages that will empower the child to live a wonderful and *full* life.

What are the *three messages* you would most want to leave with the child? Write each separate message below in the boxes.

Component 2

Shared and Supportive Leadership

OVERVIEW AND CURRENT THINKING

When PLC school staff demonstrates shared leadership, they are collaboratively sharing power, authority, and decision making. The principal and other positional leaders participate with the staff as learners and contribute democratically to decision making and guiding and supporting members of the staff to develop leadership qualities and skills. Characteristics required of these positional leaders whose school staff is operating as a PLC include the need to share authority, the ability to facilitate the work of the staff, and the capacity to participate without dominating.

In the PLC, principals (with the teachers) are learning, questioning, investigating, and seeking solutions that will lead to improved student results. The staff is consistently involved in discussing and making decisions about school issues, but with the understanding that some areas must be the purview of the principal alone. The principal actively nurtures the entire staff's development as a community, but finds opportunities for the staff to perform in leadership roles. Leadership is promoted and fostered among members of the staff who have accessibility to data and key information in order to make sound decisions.

Thus, this is not a school where the principal views only teachers and students as learners. As Roland Barth once stated, "The principal is the head learner." The principal is not the sole leader or authority in the school: these roles are shared with the staff that are actively supported in developing the attributes required of the leadership roles. The principal emerges from the "sage on stage" to the "guide on the side."

LEARNING OPPORTUNITY 2.1

Friendly Feedback for the Principal

Because of the hierarchical nature of the relationships within schools, it is the responsibility of the person with greater power to take the initiative to build and sustain trusting relationships.

—Tschannen-Moran (2004)

Outcome

The principal and staff will identify how principal leadership and participation are key in establishing schoolwide PLCs. The PLC will then create a communication/action plan to support the principal's role in the PLC.

Assumption

The principal plays a key role in assisting the PLC in finding the time, the resources, and the support for being successful and learning.

Suggested Time

1.5 hours

Materials

- Sticky notes
- Flip chart and markers
- "Leader and Learner" (see p. 58; one copy for each participant)
- "Friendly Feedback for the Principal" (see p. 62; one copy for each participant)

Learning Event

1. **Set the stage** by having each member of the PLC identify anything the principal could be doing to help the PLC become more successful in its work. Have each person write each suggestion down on a separate sticky note. They can make as many suggestions as they think is necessary.

2. On the flip-chart paper, **create** three headings: (1) Implementation, (2) Participation, and (3) Modeling Learning. Have the PLC members place their sticky notes in the column where their suggestion is making a request. If it doesn't show up in any of these three columns, you might add one called "other." When all the notes are up on the flip

chart, have the PLC members notice if there is any pattern showing up. They don't need to read any of their specific suggestions just yet. You might ask them what they think various groupings of notes mean.

3. **Invite** the PLC members to read "Leader and Learner." At the end of the reading, have each identify an important learning about the role of the principal and the implementation and sustainability of the PLC in the school.

4. **Ask** the PLC members to complete the assessment, "Friendly Feedback for the Principal." The assessment follows the ideas mentioned in the article. You might think about having the principal take the assessment prior to the PLC meeting so you can have those data available. Another option: you can work as a whole group and reach a consensus on what everyone thinks the principal has been doing in supporting the work of the PLC.

5. **Remember** this is friendly feedback for the principal, and it is how the PLC members feel supported in the implementation and sustainability of the PLC in the school. This is *not* a "gotcha" for the principal. You might think of it as a communication tool to better coordinate and sustain the learning and work of the PLC members with the principal.

6. **Provide closure** by working through the results and create a plan for enhancing the communication between the PLC and the principal and agree on next steps for supporting and sustaining the learning and work in the PLC. At this time, you might return to your list of sticky notes for additional ideas.

Future Application

The completed Communication Plan or Action Plan at the end of the assessment should be an agreement between the principal and the PLC members to support the work and learning in the PLC in a way that benefits student learning. You can use this form to enhance communication and requested action to the principal from the PLC members. Each month you might meet with the principal to report and discuss what the PLC is learning and how its work is affecting the learning of students in the school. The best way to gain the support of principals is through friendly feedback that draws on the positive as well as suggested improvements.

Notes:

LEADER AND LEARNER

Stephanie Hirsh and Shirley Hord

Preview

- Principals benefit from schoolwide professional learning communities (PLCs) with their teachers so that everyone is learning and working toward the same goal.
- Principals also find value in joining administrators' PLCs to work on their leadership and learning skills.
- Timely topics, such as investigating student performance data, are powerful organizing elements.

One of the most powerful ways for principals to extend their learning is to participate in professional learning communities (PLCs), forums that are explicitly designed to convene educators for learning so that students perform at higher levels. Principals can use PLCs to their professional advantage in two significant ways: by participating with teachers in PLCs that are designed for schoolwide learning and by working with other principals to learn specifically about school leadership and other topics.

Schoolwide PLCs

Principal leadership and participation are key to establishing schoolwide PLCs. To support learning for administrators, teachers, and students. PLCs share five research-based dimensions, shared and supportive leadership; a shared vision; supportive structural and relational conditions; intentional, collegial learning, and shared practice.

Although the principal is responsible for launching a PLC, successful principals plan how they will share guidance and leadership with the staff from its inception. Ultimately, the PLC should be a self-governing entity in which democratic participation is the norm and the principal feels comfortable sharing leadership because the PLC reflects the shared beliefs that constitute the school's vision, the second research-based element. That vision includes the purpose for which the school exists, how its members fit within that purpose, and the values upon which it is founded. Working with parents and staff members to develop a shared vision for decision making and referencing that vision often is the principal's responsibility.

The third research-based dimension is establishing supportive structural and relational conditions. At the initiation of the PLC, the principal, with staff members' cooperation, must identify the time and location where the community will meet to do its work. Finding time to

> Principal leadership and participation are key to establishing schoolwide PLCs.

meet is a real challenge, and schools and districts far and wide have found creative ways to change schedules or time usage. Another supportive condition addresses relationships—successful PLCs operate within schools where administrators, teachers, parents, and students respect, positively esteem, and trust one another. The principal has the power to solve logistical problems and provide structures to build relationships.

Establishing these structures and conditions positions the principal and staff members to focus on the work of the community. That work is just what the PLC label indicates—the professionals at the campus come together in a group, a community, for intentional, collegial learning, the fourth research-based dimension. The community must begin its work by determining what it will learn together. The staff examines multiple sources of student and staff member data to determine where they can celebrate high student performance and where unsatisfactory performance begs attention. The community of professional learners determines where they need to give time and effort to their learning, which might include new curricula, instructional strategies and approaches to student motivation, and they also determine how they will acquire and implement their new learning.

Sharing personal practice through follow up and coaching is the fifth dimension of an effective PLC. The staff members visit one another to observe. A principal or a visiting teacher might observe the practices that have been identified by a host teacher, carefully script notes, and follow up with the teacher later in the day. In this way individual staff members and the school organization as a whole improve.

Principals' Roles in the PLC

The principal plays a strong directing role at the initiation of the PLC, then steps back to support leadership opportunities and leadership development of the staff. Sharing the power, authority, and decision making with the staff can be challenging for some principals. But those who have accomplished this transmission have found it highly satisfying to have colleagues who share in the responsibilities of and accountability for improving instruction for the students of the school. One does not, of course, just turn over new roles to staff members without preparing them. From the inception of PLCs, the principal orchestrates how staff members will be prepared for new leadership roles. The principal might take full responsibility for PLC development or share it with other district administrators.

> The principal plays a strong directing role at the initiation of the PLC, then steps back to support leadership opportunities and leadership development of the staff.

Principals' levels of participation in a PLC vary. Teachers take notice of the different levels. They observe the principal who ceremoniously launches learning communities but fails to invest any individual time in the effort, they observe the principal who attends the meetings but whose actions do not demonstrate an individual investment, and they observe the principal who engages as an equal member of the community and ensures the full effect of the PLC on staff members and students.

When the PLC principal shifts from serving as the director and authority source to an individual who rolls up his or her sleeves and participates with the teaching staff, the principal has the opportunity to become a learner as opposed to solely a facilitator. When principals learn in this environment, there are additional benefits. The principal is viewed as the "head learner" who is engaged in learning and encouraging others to do likewise. He or she gains valued colleagues while discussing instructional issues that focus on students. In addition, staff involvement in school decisions and actions provides the principal with partners who help in managing and leading the school.

Principals' PLCs

Principals have other opportunities to engage in PLCs beyond their own schools. Some of these opportunities may be offered by the school system, and others are offered by external organizations. When central office staff members design professional learning for principals, they consider the context, process, and content that are most likely to address the district and individual school priorities and achieve the desired outcomes of the participants. Some districts may choose to organize principals by school demographics or experience levels. Other districts may organize PLCs by content needs or interests.

The most powerful organizer for PLCs is student performance. Principals examine data to determine specific student performance goals. Simulating the process they facilitate within their own schools, they identify what they must learn to address performance challenges. They determine a process for learning that will enable them to apply new knowledge and skills back in their schools. They create strategies for ensuring on-the-job support when needed. They identify how they will be accountable for their actions and how they will help others be accountable as well. They assess whether members are getting what they need from one another. Finally, they take time to celebrate their results and to continue a cycle of reflective planning that leads to constant improvement.

One of the better known examples of PLCs for principals focused on improved instructional practice and student learning was implemented by Anthony Alvarado in New York City (Elmore, 1997). Alvarado organized principals into PLCs to develop expertise in teaching literacy and help teachers improve their instructional skills, which led to a steady climb in student achievement over 10 years (Haycock, 1998). The process enabled the principals to facilitate instructional improvement in classrooms. Alvarado moved on to San Diego, CA, and in a study of that district, Hightower (2002) wrote:

> Alvarado's belief in the crucial role of principals as linchpins for change within schools led almost immediately to the dismantling of the area superintendent arrangement and the creation of seven heterogeneous working groups of about 25 principals each, known as Learning Communities. These were headed by principals selected for their strong instructional leadership. These instructional leaders worked closely together to design their new roles and plan their coaching work with principals. They received training from the Learning Research and Development Center (LRDC) at the University of Pittsburgh, linking them with efforts in other urban districts around the country. (p. 3)

External assistance agencies also offer principals PLC options. Some act as facilitators for one school system, and others invite principals from several school systems. External assistance facilitators help participants define their own agendas. Although the most compelling purpose is always student learning, how each group organizes adult learning can differ. Some groups may opt for book studies. Other groups may determine a learning agenda, such as literacy; develop an action plan; conduct ongoing assessments; and discuss the impact of learning on practice. In either case, the external facilitator has a responsibility to see that ground rules are established, to ensure that all members feel that the group is serving their needs, to help hold individual members accountable for the commitments they make to the other members, to provide the resources the group requires to continue its work, and to celebrate the progress of individual members within the group.

When No Child Left Behind (NCLB) was introduced in 2002, the National Staff Development Council (NSDC) launched a network of school leadership teams that were referred to affectionately as "12 under 12." Twelve schools (4 elementary, 4 middle level, and 4 high schools) convened to take a pledge to close the achievement gap in their schools—in fact, to exceed the expectations of NCLB in less than 12 years (hence 12 schools under 12 years). Twelve principals and selected teacher leaders commit to support one another in this effort. NSDC's role is not to establish the learning agenda or structure an improvement process, but to engage the participants in a facilitated process of mutual accountability. The facilitator guides them through a process of determining their schools' needs, writing measurable student goals, establishing their learning agenda, hosting semi-annual presentations on their progress, facilitating cross-school visits, and reporting results to their systems.

Eight of the original schools are still part of the network. Departing schools have been replaced by others. It is noteworthy that two principals who left their schools have rejoined the network as the principals of new schools. Two principals who were promoted in their systems have supported new principals in the network. Only two principals from the original 12 remain at their schools, yet participation has been sustained by the leadership teams. When asked what contributes to the high retention of those network members, the members report that it's the accountability and responsibility they feel toward the other members who have taken the pledge with them, knowing that their sister schools are facing similar challenges and committed to similar results, knowing that each month they have the opportunity to share their success as well as their challenges with their colleagues in "safe" conference calls; and knowing they are not in the boat alone, but are learning from a talented group of colleagues. Holding one another mutually accountable for results and learning has been the real key to this success.

> External assistance agencies also offer principals PLC options. Some act as conveners and facilitators for one school system, and others invite principals from several school systems.

Direct and Indirect Benefits

PLC structures offer tremendous benefits to principals. When principals convene PLCs, the typical isolation of staff members is reduced and they gain collegiality and the help and support of other educators in solving the hard problems of challenged learners. Most important, schools with PLCs report significant benefits for students, including lower rates of absenteeism and decreased drop-out rates. In schools with PLCs, students have exhibited greater academic gains in math, science, history and reading than in traditional schools. And, for students of all educators who are striving to reduce the gap between students from different language, cultural, and socio-economic backgrounds, student achievement gaps are narrowed.

Principals can find immense satisfaction in having all staff members assume collective responsibility for the success of all students. Everyone becomes aware of the significant influence they have on the learning outcomes of students and the roles they play in helping all students achieve expectations. Whether the principal participates in a school-based, a district-based, or a community-based PLC, the benefits will include increased satisfaction, higher efficacy, professional renewal, and support for student improvement.

References

Elmore, R. (with Burney, D.). (1997). Investing in teacher learning: Staff development and instructional improvement in community school district #2, New York City. Retrieved from www.nctaf.org/documents/archive_investing-in-teacher-learning.pdf

Haycock, K. (1998). Good teaching matters . . . a lot: How well-qualified teachers can close the gap. *Thinking K-16, 3*(2), 3–14

Hightower, A. (2002). *San Diego City schools: Comprehensive reform strategies at work* [Electronic version]. Teaching Quality Policy Briefs, 5, 1–6.

Stephanie Hirsh (Stephanie.hirsh@nsdc.org) is the executive director of the National Staff Development Council to Oxford, OH.

Shirley M. Hord (Shirley.hord@nsdc.org) is a scholar laureate for the National Staff Development Council.

FRIENDLY FEEDBACK FOR THE PRINCIPAL

Assessing the Principal's Leadership in Supporting the PLC

(Rating: 1 = not present, 2 = somewhat present, 3 = very present, 4 = exemplary)

Implementation of the PLC

Principal's Roles and Responsibilities	PLC's Assessment				Principal's Assessment			
The principal plays a leading role in launching the PLC.	1	2	3	4	1	2	3	4
The principal supports the PLC in being self-governing.	1	2	3	4	1	2	3	4
The principal points the PLC toward the school's shared vision and beliefs.	1	2	3	4	1	2	3	4
The principal provides time for the PLC to meet.	1	2	3	4	1	2	3	4
The principal provides easy access to data to support the learning in the PLC.	1	2	3	4	1	2	3	4
The principal provides needed resources to sustain the PLC in its learning.	1	2	3	4	1	2	3	4
The principal helps the PLC implement what is being learned.	1	2	3	4	1	2	3	4
The principal celebrates the successful learning that is occurring in the PLC during the year.	1	2	3	4	1	2	3	4
Total								

Participation in the PLC

Principal's Roles and Responsibilities	PLC's Assessment				Principal's Assessment			
The principal learns with other teachers in a school-based PLC.	1	2	3	4	1	2	3	4
The principal "actively" participates as an equal member in the school PLC.	1	2	3	4	1	2	3	4
The principal assists the PLC in determining what they will be learning together in order to improve student learning.	1	2	3	4	1	2	3	4
The principal encourages PLC members to share "best practices" that are making a difference for student learning.	1	2	3	4	1	2	3	4
Total								

Modeling Learning

Principal's Roles and Responsibilities	PLC's Assessment				Principal's Assessment			
The principal learns with other principals in a PLC.	1	2	3	4	1	2	3	4
The principal models continuous learning and growth for the staff, especially as an instructional leader.	1	2	3	4	1	2	3	4
The principal readily communicates to the staff what he or she is learning in the PLC or in other learning contexts.	1	2	3	4	1	2	3	4
The principal is knowledgeable and skilled in group dynamics.	1	2	3	4	1	2	3	4
Total								

Communication and Action Plan

Final Assessment

Principal's Roles and Responsibilities	PLC's Assessment	Principal's Assessment
Implementation of the PLC	Maximum total = number of PLC members $\times$ 32 = _____ Actual total = number of PLC members $\times$ total for each _____	Maximum total = number of principals $\times$ 32 = _____ Actual total = number of principals $\times$ total for each _____
Participation in the PLC	Maximum total = number of PLC members $\times$ 16 = _____ Actual total = number of PLC members $\times$ total for each _____	Maximum total = number of principals $\times$ 16 = _____ Actual total = number of principals $\times$ total for each _____
Modeling Learning	Maximum total = number of PLC members $\times$ 16 = _____ Actual total = number of PLC members $\times$ total for each _____	Maximum total = number of principals $\times$ 16 = _____ Actual total = number of principals $\times$ total for each _____

Positive feedback on how the principal has been supporting the implementation and work of the PLCs:

Suggestions for improvement in how the principal has been supporting the implementation and work of the PLCs:

Agreement on next steps for improving the success of the school's PLC:

LEARNING OPPORTUNITY 2.2

A Guide for Making Decisions

The effectiveness of any decision depends on the degree of consensus generated for it. . . . Consensus is not majority rule; it does not even imply unanimity. It is an agreement to act. No one should be allowed to take the process hostage.

—Gharajedaghi (2006)

Outcome

The PLC will differentiate decision making in order to have the greatest impact for improving student learning while doing no harm to the system as a whole.

Assumption

All decision making will have an impact on the system as a whole either in a positive way or with unintended consequences. The more clearly we can see and understand the systems in which we are working, the better we can choose the right actions to bring about desired change.

Suggested Time

1–2 hours

Materials

- "Decision Making as Gentle Action" (see p. 67; one copy for each participant)
- "A PLC Decision Tree" (see p. 69; one copy for each participant)
- Flip-chart paper and markers

Learning Event

1. **Prior to meeting**, write on a flip-chart paper the specific decisions or actions in which the group wants to actively engage in the near future. Have each decision or action posted on its own piece of flip-chart paper. Be sure to have these posted around the room so they are easy for the group to see and access.

2. **Set the stage** by asking PLC members to think of a time in their work lives when a decision was made by a leader or a group, when they were not a part of that decision, and it had a negative consequence on others. Identify a time when such a decision had a positive consequence on others. Ask the group to identify what makes the difference

between decisions that have a positive versus negative consequence, especially on those who were not part of the decision-making process.

3. **Ask** the PLC members to read the one-page overview of "Decision Making as Gentle Action." At the end of the reading, ask staff members how they want to be sensitive to others in the system before implementing any of their decisions or actions. You might make a list of these "cautionary reminders" on flip-chart paper and post them near their decisions and actions.

4. Now **take** a specific look at each of the PLC decisions or actions listed on the flip charts. Then have everyone read over "A PLC Decision Tree" (p. 69). After reading, you might ask participants to cite specific examples of decisions that have been implemented in the last few years within the school and at which level those decisions have had an impact on the system: Leaf, Branch, Trunk, or Root. This might also be a good time to refer to their own personal examples they gave during "set the stage" and determine at what level those decisions were having an impact. This is a good time to talk about how important it is for PLC leaders to understand at what level their decision or action might impact the system as a whole.

5. Depending on the size of the PLC, **have** at least two to three members work with one of the decision and action charts. Below the decision, have them create three columns with the following headers:

Type of Decision	System Impact	Decision Action

6. **Ask** PLC members to complete each of the columns by identifying the type of decision, how it might impact the system as a whole, and what decision action needs to be considered before implementing the decision.

7. **Provide closure** by having everyone report out to the whole group after everyone has completed the information for their charts. This is a good time to address any questions and to reach a consensus by the PLC in moving forward on the decision.

Future Application

This decision-making process is useful when the PLC has decided to take some kind of action based on its learning together. This process might feel like a long road to take in making a decision within the PLC. Many school environments feel very chaotic, however, because so many decisions are being made with little consideration for how those decisions might affect others and their work. This approach builds sensitivity in the system and invites deeper reflection and consideration before staff members take any action. The decision tree can be used throughout the system at an individual, group, or school level to assess impact on the system as a whole and what kind of decision action should be considered before the final decision or action is implemented.

DECISION MAKING AS GENTLE ACTION

I began to use the term, Gentle Action, several years ago to describe the creative sorts of activities and actions that could be taken when people are sensitive to the dynamics of their surrounding environment. It could be a form of minimal but highly intelligent activity that arises out of the very nature of the system under investigation.

—F. David Peat (2008)

Whenever we choose to act differently based on a decision we have made, our choosing will have an impact of some kind on the system (family, organizational, community) in which we live and work. In some cultures, a decision to act differently can be seen as a form of *violence* to the present system. In the West, we may respond strongly to the word *violence*, however, in Eastern cultures, the word *violence* is simply a form of "sensitivity" and a reminder to "pause" before engaging in any type of new action. In cultures from the East there is awareness that all things in life are integrated and connected. You cannot change one thing in a system without it having some kind of effect on the system as a whole.

A system functions the way it does because it has found a rhythm and balance (this is sometimes called feedback) based on certain habituated actions and rituals. Sometimes these actions and rituals have been in place for many years. All together they shape the identity of those who are a part of that system. So whenever a new action is invited (and sometimes it is imposed) on a current system, it violates (another word for violence) the old order to create a new one. Any new action then is going to fundamentally affect the identity of everyone within the present system. The example below is a true story that offers an illustration for how this can play out in a school:

System Decisions

A group of eighth-grade math teachers was meeting to decide what they could do to help their students be more successful on the state math test that would be given at the end of the year. Their principal had talked to them about how poorly most of the students had done on the test that previous year and that something had to change to help the students pass. The principal was open to any possible idea. The teachers met over a number of weeks and brainstormed many ideas. They finally came up with what they thought to be the perfect plan to bring the students success. They decided to offer tutoring to the students on two occasions during the week. There would be afterschool tutoring two times a week that would focus on general math skills the teachers thought every student should have. Also, there would be tutoring twice a week during the school day to target specific math skills where many students were not successful. For this to work, however, the counselor would have to pull the students from what they called non-essential classes—art, music, phys ed, etc. And, finally, for the students who were really struggling, they would place them in the same class together to focus on the remedial skills the math teachers thought the students needed in order to pass the test. The principal liked their ideas and quickly worked to put everything in place.

System Impact of Decisions

When the state test results came back at the end of the year, to everyone's surprise there was only a small improvement in the number of students who passed the test. There are obviously a number of reasons why that may have happened. However, there was another kind of impact on the system as a whole that would be revealed in years to come. The students placed in the low-level math class struggled terribly in 9th grade algebra the following year. Actually, those students struggled with their math classes right up to graduation. Also, the parents of students getting the afterschool tutoring were frustrated because their sons/daughters missed out on afterschool activities which were one of the few things that kept their children interested and engaged in school. The staff who were identified as teaching "non-essential classes" were frustrated with the principal and the math department, and did not feel valued for their contribution to the learning of the students. From that point forward, they resisted going to staff meetings and questioned the principal on all future decisions affecting the school.

F. David Peat in his book *Gentle Action, Bringing Creative Change to a Turbulent world* (2008) reminds us that our decisions and actions can sometimes produce undesirable side effects in the systems in which we are working and living. We can hold the best intentions for our actions, but if we do not see the systems in which we are choosing to act, then we may be creating more chaos than order in the long run. And Peter Senge reminds us that today's solutions can often become tomorrow's problems. It becomes then our first order of business to see the system in which we are working and then to consider how our decisions and actions may affect that system as a whole. Susan Scott, in her best-selling book *Fierce Conversations, Achieving Success at Work and in Life, One Conversation at a Time* (2002) offers a wonderful tool to assist leaders in thinking through their decisions and the impact those decisions may have on the system. Susan calls this tool a Decision Tree. This resource has been adapted to guide your decision making in the work and learning of the PLC. Use it as a guide before making any decision in the system in which you work.

Notes:

A PLC Decision Tree

Think of your PLC as a green and growing fruit-bearing tree. In order to ensure its ongoing health, countless decisions are made daily, weekly, and monthly. In making any kind of PLC decision, you might ask yourself at what level the decision being made affects the whole school as well as other staff members. According to Susan Scott (2002, p. 119),

> The analogy of root, trunk, branch, and leaf decisions indicates the degree of potential harm or good to the organization as action is taken at each level. A trunk decision isn't necessarily more important than a leaf decision. Poor decisions at any level can hurt an organization, but if you unwittingly yank a leaf off a tree, the tree won't die. A leaf decision will not kill the tree if it is poorly made and executed. A wrong action at the root level, however, can cause tremendous damage.

Type of Decision	The Decision	System Impact	Decision Action
leaf			Make the decision. Act on it. *Do not report* the action you took.
branch			Make the decision. Act on it. *Report to the principal* the action you took and its impact on a daily, weekly, or a monthly basis.

Type of Decision	The Decision	System Impact	Decision Action
trunk			Make the decision. *Get support* for your decision from the principal or district office staff before you take action.
root			*Make the decision jointly,* with input from district office staff, the principal, and other staff members. These are the decisions that, if poorly made and implemented, could cause major harm to the organization or negatively affect student learning.

Notes:

LEARNING OPPORTUNITY 2.3

Learning Conversations

We have found that people who learn to become more self-organized, using Learning Conversations within a group, find it easier to move toward internalizing the Learning Conversation.

—Sheila Harri-Augstein

Outcome

Participants will diagnose the learning conversations in our PLCs and decide what steps to take to promote learning.

Assumption

Growth and development in any group is most productive when the language, questions, and responses are enhancing learning. Sometimes groups fall into unproductive patterns.

Suggested Time

1.5 hours

Materials

- Flip chart and markers
- "Bad Behavior: What's Wrong With Us?" (download from www.marshallgoldsmithli brary.com/cim/articles_display.php?aid=363 or send it to members electronically)

Learning Event

1. **Set the stage** by inviting PLC members to identify any practices currently existing in our groups that are getting in the way of our learning. What has been tried to support a shift from an unproductive pattern to a more productive process? Point out that "Bad Behavior" was written to increase our awareness of our patterns in meetings.

2. **Review** the purpose of the PLC. Reestablish that the goal of the PLC is adult learning. Discuss the following: What are we learning about working together in our PLC? How are we learning together in our PLC?

3. **Review** the 20 flaws in "Bad Behavior: What's Wrong With Us?" Discuss which, if any, of these flaws is operating in the group or by individuals that limits our learning?

4. **Share** in small groups. Each group will decide on the most unproductive flaw(s) and print on flip chart paper. Give examples of why a particular flaw was chosen. Make a recommendation on how to reduce the negative aspects or replace it with a more productive process. Each group will present a 2-minute report of their example(s) to the larger group and their recommendations.

5. **Provide closure** by deciding as a group what recommendation(s) the group will commit to in order to increase learning.

Future Application

After this session, take 5 minutes at the end of the next two or three meetings to assess progress on making conversations and group processes more productive. Are we doing what we said we were going to do? Are meetings increasing learning among the professionals? Are there any additional behaviors we may need to change?

Notes:

LEARNING OPPORTUNITY 2.4

Planting the PLC in a Strong Culture

In study after study, where culture did not support and encourage reform, it did not happen. It is almost impossible to overstate the importance of culture and its relationship to improved student learning. You have to have the structures, a curriculum, appropriate assessments—all of that. But if you don't have a strong and healthy school culture, none of the rest will matter.

—Peterson (1998)

Outcome

The PLC will understand the importance of school culture for improving student learning and actively apply the 12 norms of school culture in their own learning work.

Assumption

Each staff member in the school is a "culture builder" who shapes the ways work gets done and learning happens, and how people treat one another. A school that is thriving in a strong school culture will have the greatest potential to affect student learning in the PLC.

Suggested Time

1.5 hours (or over two or three PLC meetings)

Materials

- Flip chart and markers
- Scissors for each person or table
- "Puzzle" (see p. 75; one copy for each participant)
- "Good Seeds Grow in Strong Cultures" (see p. 76; one copy for each participant)
- "Culture Survey for School Leaders" (see p. 84; one copy for each participant)
- "School Culture Survey: Final Assessment" (see p. 86; one copy for each participant)

Learning Event

1. **Set the stage** by sharing the following quote with the PLC members: "School culture consists of 'the beliefs, attitudes, and behaviors which characterize a school'" (Phillips, 1996, p. 1). "School culture is the shared experiences both in school and out of school (traditions and celebrations) that create a sense of community, family, and team membership. People in any healthy organization must have agreement on how to do things and what is worth doing" (Wagner, 2006).

2. **Give** each PLC member a copy of "Puzzle." and ask members to write what they see as examples or artifacts that express the culture of their school. There should be one artifact for each piece of their puzzle.

    Have the PLC members cut out their puzzle pieces and then arrange them as a whole group in what they see as like kind categories. Once the categories are established, give a name to each grouping.

    Then, ask participants what patterns or themes they see as defining characteristics of their school's culture.

3. Have everyone **read** the article by Jon Saphier and Matthew King, "Good Seeds Grow in Strong Cultures." As PLC members are reading, have them be alert for the categories they identified in the puzzle activity and see if any of them show up in Saphier and King's article.

4. **Encourage** dialogue by inviting everyone into a conversation to explore what he or she has learned. You may want to mention briefly that a dialogue is different from a discussion. A dialogue promotes deep reflection through paraphrasing and asking inquiry-based questions that open and explore the thinking of others more than inserting our own opinions. You may want to create a list of the important ideas regarding school culture on flip-chart paper.

5. After they have finished reading and dialoguing, **ask** PLC members to take the "School Culture Survey: Final Assessment" created by Jon Saphier. This survey assesses the culture in their school based on a set of behavioral norms that affect school improvement.

6. **Provide closure** by determining which norms might best support the work of the PLC. After everyone has completed the "School Culture Survey" and final assessment, give each member in the PLC three dots. Have each person place the dots on the norms that are most deserving of extra attention. Once you have found the top three norms, identify what practical next steps each member can do individually or collectively to nurture those norms so they are more present in the school and PLC.

Future Application

Investing in cultural norms and values that have an impact on student and staff learning are critical to the PLC's success. You might create a bulletin board in the staff lounge or PLC workroom that illustrates what that norm can look like when it is operating at its best. Each month, you might also check in with other PLC members to find out what changes they are noticing in the school culture as staff members focus on a particular norm.

Notes:

PUZZLE

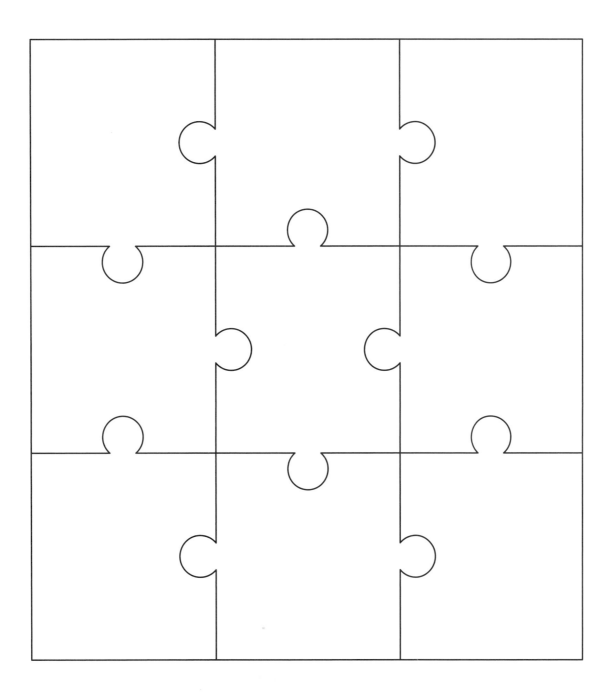

GOOD SEEDS GROW IN STRONG CULTURES

Jon Saphier and Matthew King

Regardless of the focus of particular change efforts, schools need to nurture and build on the cultural norms that contribute to growth.

School improvement emerges from the confluence of four elements: The strengthening of teacher's skills, the systematic renovation of curriculum, the improvement of the organization, and the involvement of parents and citizens in responsible school–community partnerships. Underlying all four strands, however, is a school culture that either energizes or undermines them. Essentially, the culture of the school is the foundation for school improvement, a view summarized by Purkey and Smith (1982):

We have argued that an academically effective school is distinguished by its culture: a structure, process, and climate of values and norms that channel staff and students in the direction of successful teaching and learning. . . . The logic of the cultural model is such that it points to increasing the organizational effectiveness of a school building and is neither grade-level nor curriculum specific. (p. 68)

If certain norms of school culture are strong, improvements in instruction will be significant, continuous, and widespread; if these norms are weak, improvements will be at best infrequent, random, and slow. They will then depend on the unsupported energies of hungry self-starters and be confined to individual classrooms over short periods of time. The best workshops or ideas brought in from the outside will have little effect. In short, good seeds will not grow in weak cultures.

Giving shape and direction to a school's culture should be a clear, articulated vision of what the school stands for, a vision that embodies core values and purposes. Examples of core values might be community building, problem-solving skills, or effective communication. These value commitments vary from community to community; what is important for school leaders to know is the role of values as the fuel of school improvement. If core values are the fuel, then school culture is the engine.

Figure 1 The Cultural Norms That Affect School Improvement

1. Collegiality
2. Experimentation
3. High expectations
4. Trust and confidence
5. Tangible support
6. Reaching out to the knowledge bases
7. Appreciation and recognition
8. Caring, celebration, and humor
9. Involvement in decision making
10. Protection of what's important
11. Traditions
12. Honest, open communication

The 12 Norms of School Culture

The culture norms listed in Figure 1 can be supported where they exist and built where they do not by leaders and staff. The degree to which these norms are strong makes a huge difference in the ability of school improvement activities to have a lasting—or even any—effect. Building these norms depends equally on teachers' will and commitment since good leadership alone cannot make them strong, but, without such leadership, culture cannot begin to grow or be expected to endure.

While we discuss these norms from the teachers' point of view, because teachers are culture shapers, it is important to bear in mind that there is a student culture as well. The same 12 norms apply to the culture of the school for students, but they are a direct reflection of what adults are capable of modeling among themselves.

Wherever these norms exist, they reside in teachers' and administrators' beliefs and show up in their actions. The following are hypothetical statements and represent what teachers believe and how they behave—not idle words in philosophy documents, but real actions rooted in beliefs of most of the faculty in a school with a strong culture.

1. Collegiality

In this school the professional staff help each other. We have similar challenges and needs and different talents and knowledge. When I was having problems with cliquishness among the girls, I brought it up at lunch and got some excellent ideas from the other teachers. I wasn't afraid to bring it up because I know people here are on my side. If someone thinks they hear a strange noise coming from my room, they'll stop to check it out. It isn't everyone for themselves and just mind your own business.

I think these people are darn good at what they do. I know I can learn from them and believe I have things to offer in return. Sometimes we evaluate and develop curriculum and plan special projects together, like Esther, Lorrie, and Allen doing the one week SCIS workshop for all of us this summer. Teaching each other sometimes requires more time to plan than expert-led workshops, but it allows us to work together on a significant project. Similarly our study groups—organized around topics such as cooperative learning, thinking skills, and involving senior citizens—allow us to exchange ideas. In this school we resist the notion that teaching is our second more private activity.

2. Experimentation

Teaching is an intellectually exciting activity. Around here we are encouraged by administrators and colleagues to experiment with new ideas and techniques because that is how teachers and schools improve, and we can drop experiments that do not work and be rewarded for having tried. We are always looking for more effective ways of teaching. Just last year we published "Opening Classroom Doors," a booklet with short descriptions of new ideas tried in classrooms. One teacher, for example, shared how she used jigsaw activities to do cooperative learning in social studies.

3. High Expectations

In this school the teachers and administrators are held accountable for high performance through regular evaluations. We are specifically expected to practice collegiality and to experiment with new ideas. We are rewarded when we do and sanctioned if we don't. Our continued professional development is highly valued by the school community. While we often feel under pressure to excel, we thrive on being part of a dynamic organization.

4. Trust and Confidence

Administrators and parents trust my professional judgment and commitment to improvement—no matter how effective I really am—and show confidence in my ability to carry out my professional development and to design instructional activities. We are encouraged to bring new ideas into our classes and given discretion with budgets for instructional materials.

5. Tangible Support

When I need help to improve my instruction, people extend themselves to help me with both time and resources. Indeed, when resources become scarce, professional development remains a priority. Around here

> "Cultures are built through the business of school life. It is the way business is handled that both forms and reflects the culture."

people believe the professional knowledge and skills of teachers are so important to good schooling that developing human resources is a high and continued commitment. Despite financial constraints we still have sabbaticals, summer curriculum workshops, and funds to attend professional conferences.

These first five norms have complicated and dependent relationships with one another. Little (1981) has written at length about the first three norms in her studies of "good schools." In these schools, leaders have high expectations that teachers will be collegial and experiment in their teaching. Rather than being dependent on fortuitous chemistry in a group (though it helps), collegiality is an expectation that is explicitly stated by the leader, rewarded when it happens, and sanctioned when it doesn't. Barth (1984) goes as far as to argue that "the nature of the relationships among the adults who inhabit a school has more to do with the school's quality and character, and with the accomplishments of its pupils, than any other factor." The importance of leaders being explicit about what they want and pressing for it is supported by recent work on school change (Loucks, 1983). While leaders need to be direct about what they expect, excellent leaders allow people plenty of latitude in choosing how they realize it.

My interpretation of the school effectiveness literature leads me to believe that these schools are both tightly coupled and loosely coupled, an observation noted as well by Peters and Waterman (1982) in their studies of American's best run corporations. There exists in excellent schools a strong culture and clear sense of purpose, which defines the general thrust and nature of life for their inhabitants. At the same time, a great deal of freedom is given to teachers and others as to how these essential core values are to be honored and realized. This combination of tight structure around clear and explicit themes, which represent the core of the school's culture, and of autonomy for people to pursue these themes in ways that make sense to them, may well be a key reason for their success (Sergiovanni, 1984, p. 13).

Thus, leaders might require teachers to work on expanding their repertoires of teaching skills but leave the choice of how and what up to them. Simultaneously, though, these leaders would offer tangible support—for example, one release afternoon a month—and provide a menu of options such as in-house study groups, outside speakers, tuition for attending workshops or courses, or support for individual projects.

6. Reaching Out to the Knowledge Base

There are generic knowledge bases about teaching skills and how students learn; about teaching methods in particular areas, about young people's cognitive and affective development and about each of the academic disciplines. These knowledge bases are practical, accessible, and very large. Teachers and supervisors are continually reaching out to them to improve their teaching and supervision.

There are two features of this norm we would like to highlight. The first is its aggressively curious nature. There is always more to learn, and we can respond to that understanding with energy and reach out beyond our classes or our buildings, sharing journals, attending workshops, visiting each other and other sites. A principal could model this by inviting several teachers to visit another school with him or her. Such an activity might build collegiality by bringing together teachers who don't normally work together. Indeed, as much may happen during the ride together and over lunch as happens during the visit itself.

The second feature of this norm is the reality and usefulness of these knowledge bases. The erroneous belief that there is no knowledge base about teaching limits any vision of teacher improvement. It is also isolating because in the absence of knowledge, good teaching must be intuitive; if "goodness" is unborn and intuitive, then having problems is a sign of inadequacy or too little of the "right stuff." This syndrome discourages talking about one's teaching, especially one's problems. Furthermore, if good teaching is intuitive and there's no knowledge base, what's the good of working on improvement?

But the knowledge base on teaching is very real and expanding all of the time. It tells us that there are certain things that all teachers do regardless of age group, grade, or subject. It tells us the situations or missions that all teachers have to deal with in one way or another. It also tells us what our options are for dealing with each area of teaching and that matching behaviors and techniques to specific students is the name of the game. In some cases, it even gives us guidelines for how to go about the matching.

Teachers make decisions and act to deal with numerous aspects of their instruction and relationships with students. For example, experts agree that there are dozens of ways to gain and maintain attention, several kinds of objectives (Saphier & Gower, 1982), and over 20 models of teaching (Joyce & Weil, 1980). Because there are many ways to deal with the myriad of teaching tasks, skillful teaching involves continually broadening one's repertoire in each area and picking from it appropriately to match particular students and curriculums. The knowledge base about teaching is the available repertoire of moves and patterns of action in any area available for anyone to learn, to refine, and to do skillfully.

> "Giving shape and direction to a school's culture should be a clear, articulated vision of what the school stands for, a vision that embodies core values and purposes."

Consider another knowledge base. Each subject has, in addition to the formal knowledge of its discipline, a how-to knowledge base of teaching methods and materials. Where it is the norm to consult the knowledge bases, teachers are reaching to learn new methods and examine the latest materials and not to find the single best ones, because there are no best ones. They seek to expand their repertoires so as to expand their capacity to reach students with appropriate instruction.

This particular norm, reaching out to the knowledge bases, is one of the least understood and most neglected. It is also one of the most powerful for rejuvenating an ailing school culture. In schools where the knowledge bases are cultivated, a common language for talking about instruction emerges. This language reduces the isolation commonly experienced by teachers (Lortie, 1972).

7. Appreciation and Recognition

Good teaching is honored in this school and community. The other day I found a short note from the principal in my mailbox. *When Todd and Charley were rough-housing in the hall you spoke to them promptly and firmly yet treated them maturely by explaining the whys of your intervention. It really makes our grown-up talk about respect mean something when teachers take responsibility for all kids the way you do.* He just observed that incident for a minute, yet took the time to give me feedback. (Somehow it had more impact in writing, too). Things like that make me feel there is a real value placed on what I do with students. I am recognized for my efforts and achievements in the classroom and the school.

There are many ways this message can be sent: teacher recognition as a regular feature of school committee meetings; PTA luncheons and the beginning and end of the year for faculty and staff; short notes in teachers' mailboxes from a principal who notes something praiseworthy during a walk around the building; perhaps even superior service awards written up each year in local newspapers with stipends given annually to a few teachers. Of course, underlying these efforts should be a pay scale that is at least competitive with neighboring districts.

8. Caring, Celebration, and Humor

There are quite a number of occasions when we show our caring for each other and awareness of significant events in each others' lives, as well as celebrating benchmarks in the life of the school. Estelle, for example, somehow arranges a 15-minute party with some goody for every faculty member's birthday in her building. We often have these short but satisfying little gatherings in the teacher's room before the kids come in. There is a lot of humor and laughing together in this school.

9. Involvement in Decision Making

I am included in certain meaningful decision-making processes in this school, especially when they directly affect me or my kids. That doesn't mean I am consulted on all policies or decisions; but to tell you the truth, I don't want to be—I'd never get all of my own work done. But when I am consulted, it's not a phony gesture; my input is taken seriously, and there are mechanisms open for me to raise issues. Last spring I asked the faculty advisory council to look at how kids were treating each other in the halls. That led to a faculty brainstorming session on the topic of school climate. I don't always get people to buy into my issues, or even ask them to. But when I do, the issues are treated seriously, and I am esteemed for bringing them up even if my solutions do not carry the day.

10. Protection of What's Important

Administrators protect my instruction and planning time by keeping meetings and paperwork to a minimum. In fact, we don't even have faculty meetings in the usual sense...certainly not just for business and announcements. Those needs get covered by memos and word-of-mouth contact with the principal, often in small groups like the study group on learning styles I was in last spring.

11. Traditions

There is always something special to look forward to as I scan the calendar. Be it a fair, a trip, or a science Olympiad, there are events coming up that students and teachers alike see as refreshing or challenging and a definite change of pace. Some of these traditions are rooted in ceremony, others in activity. They exist both in the curriculum as grade-level projects or activities and as recurrent events within the life of the school.

12. Honest, Open Communication

I take responsibility for sending my own messages. I can speak to my colleagues and administrators directly or tactfully when I have a concern or a beef without fear of losing their esteem or damaging our relationship. Around here people can disagree and discuss, confront and resolve matters in a constructive manner and still be supportive of each other. And I can listen to criticism as an opportunity for self-improvement without feeling threatened.

Robert Hinton captures these qualities when describing changing relationships in a Chinese village during the revolution:

> One had to cultivate the courage to voice sincerely held opinions regardless of the view held by others, while at the same time showing a willingness to listen to others and to change one's own opinion when honestly convinced of error. To bow with the wind, to go along with the crowd was an irresponsible attitude that could never lead to anything but trouble. . . . The reverse of this, to be arrogant and unbending, was just as bad. (Hinton, 1966, p. 395)

This type of communication is supported by several of the cultural norms. Difficult issues and criticism require an inner conviction that one is all right and respected by others. Appreciation and Recognition, Involvement in Decision Making, and Reaching Out to the Knowledge Bases support this kind of mutual respect.

> "The knowledge base on teaching is very real and expanding all the time. It tells us that there are certain things that all teachers do, regardless of age group, grade, or subject."

How to Build the Norms of School Culture

Sergiovanni (1984) describes five leadership forces where actions make a difference in building good schools (see Figure 2). Effective leaders have skills with which to apply each force.

Technical skills pertain to such managerial matters as scheduling and delegating; human skills include listening, group dynamics, and conflict resolution. Educational skills include knowledge about teaching and learning; symbolic skills include knowledge of and commitment to core institutional values and ways of articulating and representing them. And the cultural arena involves building norms such as the 12 discussed here. But if we are to understand what leaders do to build and maintain excellence in schools, the relationship among the five forces and arenas for action shown in Figure 2 needs expansion.

Leaders show their technical, human, and educational skills through activities that call them forth rather directly. A parents' night must be organized (technical and human), difficult meeting chaired (human), and conferences held after classroom observations (human and educational). We offer the proposition that leaders show their symbolic and culture-building skills through those same activities and not in separate activities that are exclusively symbolic or cultural (with exceptions like opening-of-school speeches that are symbolic occasions). From this perspective Sergiovanni's diagram might be redrawn as shown in Figure 3.

Figure 2 Sergiovanni's Leadership Forces that Build Good Schools

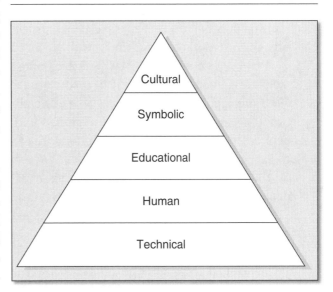

Cultures are built through the everyday business of school life. It is the way business is handled that both forms and reflects the culture. Leaders with culture-building on their minds bring an ever-present awareness of these cultural norms to their daily interactions, decisions, and plans,

Figure 3 Adapting Sergiovanni's Leadership Forces

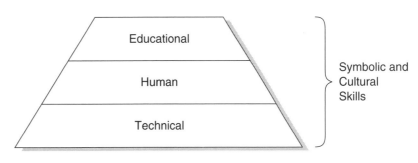

thus shaping the way events take place. Because of this dynamic, culture-building occurs simultaneously and through the way school people use their educational, human, and technical skills in handling daily events or establishing regular practices.

For example, suppose there is interest in a revised curriculum planning procedure. What would a culture-builder do in a leadership position? A sure way to prevent the crisis management of curriculum—where small numbers of parents can successfully pressure a school board, superintendent, or principal to "look into" a curriculum area such as science—is to maintain a planning process that systematically and routinely evaluates and renovates all curriculum areas. Such a system might ask parent–teacher committees to assess the existing curriculum by reviewing literature, consulting experts, and interviewing parents. Having established a curriculum's strengths and weaknesses, the committee could write a statement of philosophy to guide the next phase—the identification of new curriculums, texts, and activities, recognizing that the review process might well validate existing programs.

With the first phase of planning complete, the parents leave the committee and turn the actual development of new curriculum over to the faculty and administration. Over the next several years programs and activities are piloted and implemented, leading back to the evaluation phase in approximately five years. In this way all curriculum areas can be located on the planning cycle. While this approach to curriculum planning can be done by whole school systems, the process is especially powerful when conducted in individual schools.

A planning process such as this is itself an opportunity for infusing the cultural norms into a school. A good place to start is with a leader offering to parents and teachers Lightfoot's (1983) notion of a "consciousness of imperfection," a perspective in which we assume that any school has areas of strength and weakness and that the "good" school is distinguished by its openness to dealing with its imperfections. The school leader could use this opportunity to point out how improvements emerge from a culture that embodies norms such as our 12. She or he can then outline a process that demands experimentation by piloting new curriculum and encourages collegiality by asking teachers to work together on evaluation and design. Central to the planning is a commitment to involve stakeholders in decision making while being clear about the limits of their influence.

After completing the review, the administrator must ensure that teachers receive support to carry out their plans. For example, if a science committee recommends integrating microcomputers into science laboratories, funds need to be budgeted for purchasing equipment and training teachers. While providing support, the principal needs to emphasize the high expectations she or he has for their work. Building specific goals into teachers' formal evaluation—which should take place no less than every three years—is a useful way of making the connection between support and high expectations. Down the road a principal will want to recognize teachers' efforts by reporting to the superintendent and school board and perhaps even attaching rewards for their efforts. Our district distributes six thousand dollar service awards for recognizing teachers' contributions in a variety of areas.

The culture builders in any school bring an ever-present awareness of the 12 norms to everything they do in the conduct of daily business. It is this awareness and commitment to culture building that is more important than any single activity or structure in the school organization. Once we are clear about what the important norms of a strong culture are, the activities and forms through which we build them are legion.

If we are serious about school improvement and about attracting and retaining talented people to school careers, then our highest priority should be to maintain reward structures that nurture adult growth and sustain the school as an attractive workplace. A strong culture is crucial to making schools attractive workplaces. If the norms we have outlined are strong, the school will not only be attractive, it will be energized and constantly improving.

References

Barth, R. S. (1980). *Run school run.* Cambridge, MA: Harvard University.

Barth, R. S. (1984). Sandboxes and honeybees. *Education Week,* May 1.

Deal, T. E., & Kennedy, A. A. (1982). *Corporate cultures.* Reading, MA: Addison Wesley.

Hinton, R. (1966). Fanshen, New York: Vintage.

Joyce, B., & Weil, M. (1980). *Models of teaching.* Englewood Cliffs, NJ: Prentice Hall.

Lightfoot, S. (1983). *Good high schools: Portraits of character and culture.* New York: Basic.

Little, J. W. (1981). "School Success and Staff Development in Urban Desegregated Schools: A summary of Recently Completed Research." Paper presented at the annual meeting of the American Education Research Association, Los Angeles, April.

Lortie, D. C. (1972). *School teacher.* Chicago: University of Chicago.

Loucks, S. F. (1983, November). "At Last: Some Good News From a Study of School Improvement." *Educational Leadership 41,* 4–9.

Peters, T. J., & Waterman, R. H., Jr. (1982). *In search of excellence.* New York, Harper & Row.

Purkey, S. C., & Smith, M. S. (1982, December). Too soon to cheer? Synthesis of research on effective schools. *Educational Leadership, 41,* 64–69.

Saphier, J. D., & Gower, R. (1982). *The skillful teacher.* Carlisle, MA: Research for Better Teaching.

Sergiovanni, T. (1984, November). Leadership and excellence in schooling. *Educational Leadership, 41,* 4–13

Notes:

CULTURE SURVEY FOR SCHOOL LEADERS

Behavioral Norms: Qualities of the Environment that Leaders Experience

Rate each item 1–5 (1—almost never, 2—less often than not, 3—about half the time, 4—more often than not, 5—almost always).

Collegiality					
1. We talk in concrete and precise terms about things we are trying in our leadership roles.	1	2	3	4	5
2. We have productive observations of one another.	1	2	3	4	5
3. We teach each other things we know about leading.	1	2	3	4	5
4. We all recognize that leading is inherently difficult and ask for and give assistance for problems with administrative issues. And we know we'll get it without being judged.	1	2	3	4	5
Experimentation					
5. Other administrators encourage me and back me up when I try new things.	1	2	3	4	5
High Expectations					
6. Good leading is taken seriously here. This shows up in serious attention to administrative evaluation and letting me know clearly how I stand in relation to the expectations of the district. I get prompt and useful feedback.	1	2	3	4	5
Reaching Out to Knowledge					
7. This is a curious school system. We are always searching for new and improved ways to educate.	1	2	3	4	5
Appreciation and Recognition					
8. There is a close relationship in this school system between job performance and recognition of that performance.	1	2	3	4	5
Trust					
9. I feel trusted and encouraged to make administrative decisions on my own . . . and my superior backs me up when I do.	1	2	3	4	5

Caring, Celebration, and Humor					
10. We enjoy being with and around each other. We offer comfort and help when needed and join in celebration together.	1	2	3	4	5
Protecting What's Important					
11. We are protected from unreasonable demands on our time and energy that interfere with contact time with students and teachers.	1	2	3	4	5
12. Meetings are worthwhile and productive.	1	2	3	4	5
Traditions					
13. We have annual events and ceremonies we look forward to each year.	1	2	3	4	5
Tangible Support					
14. Priorities for use of money and time show me that professional development is a top priority.	1	2	3	4	5
Decision Making					
15. I feel our decision-making processes are productive and efficient.	1	2	3	4	5
16. I feel I am consulted about decisions to be made in this school system and that I am listened to and can influence policy.	1	2	3	4	5
Frank, Civil and Open Communication					
17. People speak honestly but respectfully to one another. We are not afraid to disagree and can do so without jeopardizing our relationships.	1	2	3	4	5
18. Conflicts between individuals are resolved quickly and intelligently.	1	2	3	4	5
19. The information flow keeps me informed about what's going on in the school system.	1	2	3	4	5
Initiative					
20. Administrative council members show initiative in developing new ideas for the school system and seeing them come to life.	1	2	3	4	5

Used with permission from Jon Saphier, Research for Better Teaching.

SCHOOL CULTURE SURVEY: FINAL ASSESSMENT

Culture building requires that school leaders give attention to the informal, subtle, and symbolic aspects of school life which shape the beliefs and actions of each employee within the system.

—William Cunningham

For each norm/value that you score a 4 or 5, please provide a recent example of how that norm is demonstrated through individual or organizational behavior.

Culture Norm/Value	Rating	Recent Example
Collegiality (professional collaboration on educational issues)	20 Max. _____	
Experimentation (interest in exploring new, not yet proven techniques)	5 Max. _____	
Reaching out to the knowledge base (use of research, reading of professional journals, workshops, etc.)	5 Max. _____	
Appreciation and recognition (acknowledgment of quality student/staff work and effort)	5 Max. _____	
Caring—Celebration—Humor	5 Max. _____	
Traditions (rituals and events that celebrate and support core school values)	5 Max. _____	
High expectations (a pervasive push for high performance for students and teachers)	5 Max. _____	
Protection of What's Important (school goals and priorities)	10 Max. _____	
Tangible support (financial and material assistance that supports teaching/learning)	5 Max. _____	
Professional respect (I feel trusted and encouraged to make instructional decisions on my own)	5 Max. _____	
Decision making (decision-making processes are fair and legitimate)	10 Max. _____	
Communication (honest and open)	15 Max. _____	
Initiative (staff members show initiative in developing new ideas)	5 Max. _____	

LEARNING OPPORTUNITY 2.5

Positive Deviance

It's easy to come up with new ideas; the hard part is letting go of what worked for you two years ago, but will soon be out-of-date.

—Roger von Oech

Outcome

Learners will identify "positive deviants" in their schools; i.e., those staff members whose students show above-average learning and progress. Learners will collect examples of how these professionals are producing better results with or for students and create opportunities to share and implement those examples schoolwide.

Assumption

There are staff members whose students are demonstrating higher proficiency than the norm. Better results are already happening with the very students about whom some staff say, "It can't be done." Finding out what these professionals are doing is an imperative if a learning community is to show increased results and to distribute successful instructional strategies.

Suggested Time

Two meetings of 1–1.5 hours

Materials

- Flip chart and markers
- Student performance data
- "Story of Positive Deviance" (see p. 89; one copy for each participant, or go to www.fast-company.com, type in Positive Deviance for the article, then send it to members electronically)

Learning Event

1. **Set the stage** by asking participants to share one teaching practice that produces the best results for their students. Make sure everyone has a chance to speak.

2. **Download** on a computer or distribute the article Positive Deviance. How did Jerry Sternin find out what the major factors were in raising healthy children in Vietnam? How will the professionals in the PLC find out what the major factors are of getting higher student results?

3. **Ask** participants to look at the student data and identify those classes where students are making the best progress. Which staff members are producing the best results?

4. **Decide** who will interview the staff members who are getting the best results to find out what strategies they are using.

5. **Ask** participants to develop a list of strategies they found in the interviews and record on flip chart paper. Review the list and decide which strategies are the most promising possibilities for your school, department, or grade level.

6. **Determine** how to teach the strategies to additional staff. This may include demonstrations at department meetings, schoolwide meetings, district meetings, and so on. Any staff member can contribute a strategy to the group.

7. **Invite** participants to select one or more of the possibilities and create a plan for implementing the new strategy they have learned.

8. **Collect** examples of strategies that work, and collect student data to determine which strategies are the most effective with students in the classroom.

9. **Determine** who in the group will communicate the strategies that are producing the best results to others in the school. That PLC member is to report the strategies to the school staff. What did the staff member(s) or department(s) learn that increases student learning? What are the recommendations for this new strategy as ways to teach students? What difference will this make for students in the long term?

10. **Provide closure** by creating a list of *positive deviant* strategies in a journal or on the Web for schoolwide access. How might this contribute to the district knowledge base?

Future Application

What other resources are there to expand positive deviant applications? Do an Internet search for work by the late Jerry Sternin of Tufts University. An additional resource for *amplifying positive deviance* can be found at www.nsdc.org. How will we celebrate new learning for staff members? How will we celebrate new learning for students?

Notes:

STORY OF POSITIVE DEVIANCE

As part of an international "Save Our Children" program, Jerry Sternin was commissioned in the 1990s to go to Vietnam to help combat starvation. When Jerry got off the plane in Hanoi, the officials told him he had one month to come up with something that would help the starving children or they would send him back to America. Jerry knew he had to come up with questions, not answers.

We asked, "Why not answers?" Jerry replied, if we were native Vietnamese, would we believe a white person from America would have the answer? Ah, good point. How many times do consultants go in with an answer and the staff says, "You can't do that with our students or in our community."

So Jerry asked, "Are there healthy kids living in these villages?" The officials said they didn't care about those kids: they wanted help for the malnourished. Jerry said, "Why are there healthy kids living in the same conditions as the unhealthy kids?" The officials didn't know. Jerry asked, "Can you identify the healthy kids?" The officials said, "Yes," and proceeded to find healthy kids. They recorded data about height, weight, vital signs, and so on.

The officials came back with a list of healthy kids. Jerry asked, "Do any of these children have access to outside resources?" An example of outside resource would be if an uncle in a neighboring village was a pharmacist, that child might get medicine that other children would not have access to. The officials didn't know the answer.

The officials came back with a list of children who were healthy and had no access to outside resources. Jerry then asked, "What are the families doing different for these kids?" Again, the officials were stumped but committed to talking to the parents to find out if there were any differences.

The officials came back with a list of practices they were using. One was that the parents of healthy kids were feeding their children four times a day rather than the normal two times a day. Small children, small stomachs, and food moves through their system faster. Another practice was the parents of healthy kids fed their children the shrimps and crabs that accumulated on the ends of rice stalks. That increased protein in the system. Unhealthy children were eating mainly rice.

Two things Jerry and the officials did not do were to make a list of healthy nutritional practices, make posters, and display those posters around the community. Another thing Jerry and the officials did not do was to collate the data, duplicate it, and pass it out to everyone in the village.

What Jerry and the officials DID do was to convene conversations with parents of healthy children and parents of unhealthy children and let the information pass between the parents in the community. Those parents are going to trust those who they live with, work with, and with whom they are familiar.

How might a PLC be like the conversations convened to help the starving children in Vietnam?

Notes:

Adapted from a story told by Jerry Sternin to the NSDC Board of Trustees (July 2004)

LEARNING OPPORTUNITY 2.6

Distributed Leadership

There is no limit to what you can do if you don't care who gets the credit.

—Unknown

Outcome

Participants will determine the degree of shared leadership in their PLC and implement steps to increase shared leadership, if necessary.

Assumption

Leadership is usually defined as an administrator function, focusing almost exclusively on the principal and assistant principals. There exists a great deal of talent in all groups—teachers, administrators, paraprofessionals, and so on—in every school. High-performing cultures find, share, and develop leadership talent that can increase learning.

Suggested Time

1.5 hours

Materials

- Flip chart and markers
- pp. 10–11 of *Leading Professional Learning Communities: Voices From Research and Practice* (Hord & Sommers, 2008)
- "Notes From Distributed Leadership" (see p. 92; one copy for each participant)

Learning Event

1. **Set the stage** by asking learners to define leadership, as they understand the term. Record these on the flip chart tablet. Ask participants to turn to pages 10–11 in Hord and Sommers (2008), and to compare their thoughts with the Shared Leadership description in the book.

2. **Read** the "Notes From Distributed Leadership" by Spillane. Use the questions provided in the notes to guide the conversation. Invite the group to answer, "How has this information, the Shared Leadership segment in the book, and the discussion enhanced your current definition of shared leadership?" Make additions or corrections on the flip chart paper that will help define the term "Shared Leadership."

3. **Discuss** the definition of shared leadership, noted above; as a group, determine what leadership responsibilities are necessary for a high-performing PLC.

4. **Write** on flip chart paper the major responsibilities and behaviors we will see and hear from the leaders in our PLCs. Write on flip-chart paper the major responsibilities and the behaviors the PLCs will see and hear from the participants in the PLC.

5. **Provide closure** by sharing the leadership and participant responsibilities and behaviors with the whole staff via posters, e-mail, notes, and so on to assist in shared understanding among the staff.

Future Application

Review these responsibilities and behaviors at least once a semester to assess the implementation of agreed-upon responsibilities and behaviors. Is there an area of responsibility missing? Are there areas of overlap? Make necessary modifications.

Notes:

NOTES FROM DISTRIBUTED LEADERSHIP

James P. Spillane

Distributed leadership is about the practice of leadership. Distributed leadership is not about Superman and Wonder Woman. It is about the joint interactions of school leaders, followers, and aspects of their situation—tools and routines. It is the collective interactions among leaders, followers, and their situation that are paramount.

Leaders are agents of change. Leadership is defined as a relationship of *social influence.* Leading schools requires multiple leaders. Two thoughts:

1. Leaders practice together cofacilitating the professional development meetings.

2. Leaders not only influence followers, but also are influenced by them.
   Coleadership happens when "power and responsibility are dispersed."
   Expecting one person to single-handedly lead efforts to improve instruction in a complex organization, such as a school, is impractical.

Discuss leadership as a set of organizational functions rather than tying leadership to a particular administrative position. Consider these four questions:

1. Who takes responsibility for leadership work?

2. How are these responsibilities arranged?

3. How do these arrangements come to pass?

4. How do individuals get constructed as influential leaders?

Question: How are leadership responsibilities arranged in our organization?

- Division of labor
- Co-performance
- Parallel performance

Questions: Teachers base their beliefs on human, cultural, social, and economic capital. Which of the following are most important in our organization? Who are the leaders in each of these forms of capital? Who are the leaders in more than one of the following?

- *Human capital* involves a person's knowledge, skills, and expertise.
- *Cultural capital* refers to a person's way of being and doing, interactive styles that are valued in particular contexts.
- *Social capital* refers to a person's social networks or connections but also concerns the prevalence of norms, e.g., trust, collaboration, and a sense of obligation among individuals in an organization.
- *Economic capital* includes money and other material resources, including books, curricular materials, and computers, among other things.

From Spillane, J. (2006). *Distributed leadership.* San Francisco: Jossey-Bass.

Component 3

Structural Conditions

OVERVIEW AND CURRENT THINKING

In our original book, *Leading Professional Learning Communities,* we approached structural conditions and relational conditions as one entity: supportive conditions. Supportive conditions provide the infrastructure and requirements of the when, where, and how the staff can come together as one unit to learn, make decisions, and implement new practices.

We have now chosen to address these two supportive conditions separately, for they seem to represent very discrete concepts and variables in the life and operation of the PLC. Most assuredly, physical factors such as the time and location for the community to meet are critical needs for the PLC. Without these conditions, there can be no community. (One might argue here about online PLCs, which we have not taken into our lexicon at this time, although the authors are becoming involved and learning about this context for the PLC—stay tuned.)

But there is more to structural or physical or inorganic conditions than time, although the importance of time has led us to give considerable attention to it in the learning opportunities in this book. Other structural factors include the following:

- The size of the school and the proximity of the staff to each other. If the staff exceeds 30–35 individuals, it would seem wise to divide them in some meaningful way in order to make sharing "airtime" and conversation productive. If the staff members are widely separated or distanced from each other, this creates issues of interaction and collaboration.
- Communication procedures. Consistently, staff members in schools complain about the lack of shared information and communication. Using message boards in the staff lounge and workroom, daily e-mail messages to teachers' desks, and weekly newsletters that go to staff or parents are typical and standard means by which efforts are made to keep staff informed. And they can work well, if someone has the designated task of coordinating the text and managing the operations that support effective exchange of information.

- Resources. There is every reason to believe the PLC will require access to multiple avenues of information. If the PLC is to engage in learning new and deeper content, new instructional strategies, or unique approaches to motivating and engaging students, there will be needs for books, journals, CDs, and other materials. Additional human resources also may be required to support a PLC.

- Schedules and structures that reduce staff isolation are vital so staff members can convene to do their work. Policies at the district and state levels that foster collaboration and provide for staff learning should be "on the books." These structural conditions should be considered and planned for in advance of launching the PLC. Otherwise, there will be widespread frustration and discontent.

LEARNING OPPORTUNITY 3.1

Time and Other Essential Ingredients

It takes nine months to make a baby, no matter how many people you put on the job.

— American saying

Outcome

Learners will identify the structural needs of the community, with suggestions for how these requirements may be accessed.

Assumption

The basic needs of time, space, resources, and communication structures must be in place so that the learning community may function productively. Planning for these is imperative if a learning community is expected to be launched and thrive.

Please note: This learning opportunity, we believe, is an appropriate target for (1) staff development chairs at the school or district levels; for (2) school leaders, including the principal and assistant principals, grade team chairs, department chairs, and other teacher leaders; and for (3) the learning community members. How the learning opportunity will be applied by each of these three different "users" will be different and modified based on their discretion.

Suggested Time

1–1.5 hours

Materials

- Flip chart and markers
- pp. 51–58 of *Leading Professional Learning Communities: Voices From Research and Practice* (Hord & Sommers, 2008)

Learning Event

1. **Set the stage** by asking participants to identify the time when the grade-level teams or academic departments of the schools and the whole faculty staff of schools currently meet. Record on flip-chart pads. (It has been recommended that the professional learning teams meet once a week, and the whole faculty community meets once a month at a minimum. Meeting twice would be more effective in maintaining the schools' subparts in alignment.) Is time for meeting a challenge for the schools? If so,

2. **Invite** the participants (district or campus-based leaders) to meet this charge for developing a structure—time and place—for initiating a PLC (if a PLC has not yet been introduced) by

referring them to Hord & Sommers (2008, p. 53–54, and p. 56, Table 3.1). Ask participants to review the list and suggest the most promising possibilities for their particular setting. If the PLC has begun to meet, but time comes up as an issue in the PLC meetings, follow these same directions with members of the PLC.

Finding a place for the whole staff to meet is sometimes difficult. Refer to Hord and Sommers (2008, pp. 54–58). Invite participants to make a quick floor plan of their school and to mark spaces that might accommodate the whole staff. We like the idea of rotating the meetings of the community around teachers' classrooms (Hord & Sommers, 2008, p. 57).

Note: Valerie Von Frank's collection of articles (Von Frank, V. [Ed.]. [2008]. *Finding time for professional learning.* Oxford, OH: National Staff Development Council.), originally published primarily in the *Journal of Staff Development*, is a goldmine of ideas. Participants should be directed to it for review of the various chapters and their content.

3. **Direct** participants to select one of their possibilities (one that addresses their particular issue) and create a plan for implementing it and a means for assessing how well it worked.

4. **Review** the communication structures reported in Hord & Sommers (2008, pp. 51–53). One of the most pervasive complaints heard in all organizations, and the PLC is no exception, is the lack of information and "knowing." Invite participants to place a star by each communication idea, for their second review and consideration later.

5. **Create** an inventory of all material resources, such as journals focused on school improvement, and so on. Organize a professional library of these periodicals and books, videotapes and CDs, DVDs, and other reference resources. Locate these items in a readily accessible place for the staff. Consideration should be given to subscribing to various journals that can provide recent research and expert advice about school change processes and products.

6. **Imagine** that the district has created a districtwide schedule that supports all schools by providing time for the PLC. Imagine that the administrators and teachers in the schools begin to meet, but have not a clue about what to do in the meeting. There should not be the assumption that if time is provided, it will be used wisely. The staff has never met for PLC work and thus will need guidance. Refer to Learning Opportunity 3.4, "The Learning Community's WORK (p. 110)". Materials cited in that learning opportunity make clear what the PLC should be doing and sets expectations for them. Norms for the meetings should be identified, so that again everyone is clear about expectations.

7. **Providing closure** is only possible when issues about time have been identified and examined, resources (such as books noted in the material section) have been explored, and possible resolutions articulated. All these actions will depend on which scenario noted above pertains to the participants: (1) a PLC has not been initiated, and school or district leaders are preparing for the PLC "launch" by scheduling time; (2) the PLC has started, but time has not been carefully identified, thus this issue is taken to the PLC members for resolution; or (3) the district has provided time, but the PLCs do not know what to do with it.

Requests of the participants were made to plan for implementing their resolution. These plans now should be shared across pairs of groups, with feedback invited that could improve the plans.

Future Application

Two weeks should be provided for initiating implementation of the plans created in the session. The plan should be clearly committed to a written document, and with a report of progress of the implementation, should be shared via one of the school's communication structures. Progress should be applauded in some celebratory way.

Notes:

LEARNING OPPORTUNITY 3.2

Assessing the Effectiveness of PLC Meetings

Structure meetings so that all become capable of acting beyond the capacity of any one person. We identify a successful meeting by a group's increased capability to self-manage their own problem solving and decision making. . . .The more you manage the conditions under which people meet, the less you will need to manage their meeting behavior.

—Weisbord & Janoff (2007)

Outcome

The PLC will assess the effectiveness of their meetings and explore options for improvement.

Assumption

The sustainability of a highly effective professional learning committee is dependent on how learning work gets done when PLC members meet with each other.

Suggested Time

1.5 hours (This will take place over two consecutive meetings. You might also consider gathering this data at least two times during the year.)

Materials

- "Professional Learning Community: Meeting Reflection" (see p. 100; one copy for each participant)
- Flip chart and markers

Learning Event

First Meeting

1. **Set the stage** by asking PLC members to tell the person sitting next to him or her about a meeting he or she attended in the past that felt productive, was a good use of time, and where something significant happened at the end of the meeting. At the end of everyone sharing their stories, ask them what they think happened that made that particular meeting successful.

2. **Invite** staff members to complete the meeting reflection form at the end of a PLC meeting and tally their results on the next page.

3. **Ask** PLC members to reveal how they rated the effectiveness of the meeting. You might also have the following info posted on large flip-chart paper and place a check mark for each person in the appropriate level.

    _____0–7

_____8–16

_____17–24

4. **Ask** PLC members what they think is the reason(s) for how most of them perceived the effectiveness of the meeting.

5. **Invite** staff members to offer a number of specific requests for how PLC meetings might be improved in the future. Their requests should focus around the eight focus areas that were referenced for determining a successful PLC meeting. Their requests would be used to open the following PLC meeting.

Second Meeting

1. **Prepare** for meeting. Before PLC members arrive, have eight pieces of flip-chart paper posted in the room. At the top of each flip chart, reference one of the eight focus areas for assessing the effectiveness of a PLC meeting.

2. **Ask** everyone at the very beginning of the meeting to find a flip chart and post their request(s) for improving future PLC meetings. After all the requests have been posted, give each member three dots and have them identify three requests that they think could make the greatest difference for improving the future success of PLC meetings.

3. **Provide closure** by asking the PLC to establish meeting norms where most of the dots are placed. We suggest you establish only three or four norms so they have a better chance of being managed and practiced during the PLC meeting. Before moving on, ask each member if these are norms they are willing to be personally accountable for in future meetings. If they are, place the norms on large flip-chart paper so they can be posted in the PLC meeting room. If staff members are having difficulty with some of the norms, you may have to rewrite the norms so they feel doable and appropriate to all participants. The following are examples of meeting norms you might see posted in a PLC room.

   o We will first inquire about another person's thinking before offering our own ideas.
   o We will identify specific action items at the end of each meeting and follow up on them at the next meeting.
   o We will use student learning data to guide our own learning and discovery.

Future Application

You might place the meeting norms you want to give more attention to on each PLC meeting agenda. As a check, ask members how well they think the PLC did in manifesting those norms during the meeting. The results could then be tallied over the next couple of meetings to assess application and improvement of your identified meeting norms.

Meeting Norms

We will first inquire about another person's thinking before offering our own ideas.	0	1	2	3	4
We will identify specific action items at the end of each meeting and follow up on them at the next meeting.	0	1	2	3	4
We will use student learning data to guide our own learning and discovery.	0	1	2	3	4

PROFESSIONAL LEARNING COMMUNITY

Meeting Reflection

Bad meetings almost always lead to bad decisions, which is the best recipe for mediocrity.

—Lencioni (2004)

To what degree did our meeting	Not at all	Minimally	Adequately	Effectively
1. Help to promote a culture of learning?	0	1	2	3
2. Establish and nurture trust between all PLC members?	0	1	2	3
3. Respect the use of time in having meeting outcomes and an agenda that was sized correctly for what needed to happen?	0	1	2	3
4. Promote a spirit of inquiry individually and collectively by paraphrasing others and inviting questions that explored the thinking of others?	0	1	2	3
5. Support PLC members to make connections (both big picture connections and networking or partnerships)?	0	1	2	3
6. Assist in identifying important areas for learning or inquiry and to find ways to transfer the learning into making a difference for student learning?	0	1	2	3
7. Provide a supportive structure for everyone to feel heard and diverse viewpoints valued and honored?	0	1	2	3
8. Assist in nurturing and promoting the sustainability of the PLC?	0	1	2	3

Rating the Effectiveness of Our PLC Meeting

- ❏ 0–7:   Our PLC meeting did not feel useful or productive, and it was not respectful of my time.

- ❏ 8–16:   Our PLC meeting was useful and yet something needs to happen for meetings to be better.

- ❏ 17–24: Our PLC meeting was very productive and supported learning individually as well as collectively.

Making a Specific Request for Improving Future PLC Meetings

In order to improve future PLC meetings, reference one or more of the focus areas below and make a specific request to PLC members for improving future meetings. An example might be, *Please have action items identified and listed before the next meeting and to send out the agenda one week prior to the meeting.*

1. Promoting a culture of learning by . . .

2. Establishing and nurturing trust between all PLC members by . . .

3. Respecting the use of time by . . .

4. Promoting a spirit of inquiry individually and collectively by . . .

5. Supporting PLC members to make connections by . . .

6. Identifying important areas for learning/inquiry and transferring our learning into making a difference in student learning by . . .

7. Providing a supportive structure for everyone to feel heard and diverse viewpoints valued and honored by . . .

8. Promoting the sustainability of the PLC by . . .

Adapted from the work of Louise Stoll. Document retrieved January 2, 2009, from http://www.thegrid.org.uk/leadership/programmes/conferences/documents/EPLC_profile.doc

LEARNING OPPORTUNITY 3.3

Assessment for PLC Development

In times of change, learners inherit the earth, while the learned find themselves beautifully equipped to deal with a world that no longer exists.

—Eric Hoffer

Outcome

Participants will diagnose their PLC's development and prescribe assessment-based support for it.

Assumption

Growth and development of any organization is most productive when appropriate support is provided—i.e., support that is based on periodic assessment.

Suggested Time

1.5 hours

Materials

- Flip chart and markers
- pp. ix and 9 of *Leading Professional Learning Communities: Voices From Research and Practice* (Hord & Sommers, 2008)
- "Professional Learning Communities Observation Tool" (see p. 104; one copy for each participant)
- "School Professional Staff as Learning Community Questionnaire" (see p. 106; one copy for each participant)

Learning Event

1. **Set the stage** by asking learners across the large group to recall the research-based components of a PLC. Record these on the flip-chart tablet, including all responses, whether or not they are accurate. Then invite participants to review page 9 in Hord and Sommers (2008) to corroborate what they have listed on the flip chart and possibly revise that list.

2. **Review** the purpose of the PLC by inviting table groups to discuss the purpose and report after 3 minutes. Refer to Hord and Sommers (2008, p. ix) to find Andy Hargreaves's statement about what the PLC is meant to be (second sentence).

3. **Challenge** the groups (those from the same school teams, or whole school groups) to determine where their PLC stands in terms of its purpose (compare with Hargreaves), and the degree to which their PLC has matured vis-à-vis the research-based components. Ask for evidence about their assessment.

4. **Distribute** copies of "Professional Learning Communities Observation Tool" and "School Professional Staff as a Learning Community Questionnaire." Review the directions on the instruments and explain how to use the forms. Invite participants to fill out one each of the two forms for each PLC. Learners will analyze their data, noting strong areas of their PLCs and areas in need of attention. Each group will present a 2-minute report of their findings to the larger group.

5. **Provide closure** by instructing each group to create a written plan for addressing and providing intervention for their PLC in the area(s) in need of attention. "Neighbor" groups (in the session) will solicit and share feedback with each other.

Future Application

Back at their schools, the groups will implement their plan, utilizing whatever amount of time is required for the intervention. After the intervention has been in place, a reasonable time to be effective, participants should use the instruments again to determine if change and improvement has occurred. Depending on the findings, celebrate or revisit the assessment and prescription activities.

Notes:

This learning opportunity was created by Cathy Kinzer, assistant professor at New Mexico State University, and Shirley M. Hord, Scholar Laureate, National Staff Development Council.

PROFESSIONAL LEARNING COMMUNITIES OBSERVATION TOOL

Date: _____

School: _____

Grade: _____

Rubric: PLC Observations occur over time to note patterns. Use this tool each time with written descriptions. (Informal interviews and questions are useful to document the PLC). The questions for each element serve only as examples. Determine a rating for each element even if it is not observed at that PLC.

1. Never   2. Occasionally   3. Most of the time   4. Always   NA. Unable to determine

Structures are established at a campus for Professional Learning Communities that are situated within a broader district learning organization.	**Structure** provides consistent time (weekly, etc.) within the school day for ongoing focused and sustained, purposeful, and professional learning.	**Structures** are provided for the application of learning through modeling, team teaching, observations, etc.	**Structured** time is provided for across grade level, or specific teams, or subject areas.	**Structures** for learning include skillful facilitation, teacher driven agendas, protocols, or topics of study related to improving teaching and learning.
• Is the PLC situated in a district learning organization?	• What evidence is there that the PLC has purposeful sustained professional learning?	• Are teachers collaborating in, observing, teaching, reflecting, and revising lessons based on students' learning?	• Are learning conversations occurring in different teacher/leader configurations?	• What guides purposeful, focused PLC learning?
A Culture of collaboration is focused on improving curriculum, assessment, and instruction to promote student learning (for example, developing formative assessments or defining the content and skills students need to learn based on the standards).	**A Culture** of collaborative inquiry, reflection, and questioning exists to explore, to exchange ideas, to learn through their practice with others, with stated high expectations and explicit goals for strengthening teaching and learning.	**A Culture** of learning is established through reflective dialogue and professional communication structures within and between PLCs.	**The Culture** provides for articulating and implementing norms for productive working relationships to solve problems of practice. There is a focus on relational strengths such as honesty, respect, and caring.	**The Culture** provides for building a professional knowledge base through reading, researching, sharing practical aspects of teaching, and connecting to the broader educational community to develop the professional knowledge needed for effective teaching.

• Do teachers have a defined process for learning through student work?	• How do teachers utilize the agreed upon learning goals to study their teaching practices?	• In what ways do PLCs collaborate and share their learning?	• Do the participants utilize relational strengths and norms or protocols for building and interacting in a constructive learning space?	• Do participants have processes and shared values for building their professional knowledge?
A Learning Community builds educators' knowledge, skills, and pedagogy within the context of teaching to meet students' learning needs.	**A Learning Community** develops common vision, goals, and theory of action to attain the shared learning goals that are revisited and refined through the use of data and experience.	**A Learning Community** identifies and studies the content and processes that are problematic for themselves and their students.	**The Learning Community** participants focus on access and equity for students in learning (including ELL and SPED) and develop the expertise to meet students' learning needs.	**The Learning Community** is supported through external and internal leadership to focus on a common shared purpose through collaborative improvement of teaching, leading, and learning.
• In what ways do teachers improve students' learning through studying their professional practices?	• How do teachers enact a shared instructional vision?	• What strategies do teachers utilize to learn their content to promote student understanding?	• How do teachers develop their capacity to support all learners?	• How does leadership support improvement in teaching and learning?

Notes:

Used with permission from Cathy J. Kinzer, Mathematics Educator, New Mexico State University, Las Cruces, NM.

SCHOOL PROFESSIONAL STAFF AS LEARNING COMMUNITY QUESTIONNAIRE

DATE: _____

NAME: _____

SCHOOL: _____

> ***Directions:*** This questionnaire concerns your perceptions about your school staff as a learning organization. There are no right or wrong responses. Please consider where you believe your school is in its development of each of the five numbered descriptors shown in bold-faced type on the left. Each sub-item has a five-point scale. On each scale, circle the number that best represents the degree to which you feel your school has developed.

1. School administrators participate democratically with teachers, sharing power, authority, and decision making.

1a.

5	4	3	2	1
	Although there are some legal and fiscal decisions required of the principal, school administrators consistently involve the staff in discussing and making decisions about school issues.	Administrators invite advice and counsel from staff and then make decisions themselves.	Administrators never share information with the staff nor provide opportunities to be involved in decision making.	

1b.

5	4	3	2	1
	Administrators involve the entire staff.	Administrators involve a small committee, council, or team of staff.	Administrators do not involve any staff.	

2. The staff shares visions for school improvement that have an undeviating focus on student learning, and these visions are consistently referenced in the staff's work.

2a.

5	4	3	2	1
	Visions for improvement are discussed by the entire staff such that consensus and a shared vision result.	Visions for improvement are not thoroughly explored; some staff members agree and others do not.	Visions for improvement held by the staff members are widely divergent.	

	5	4	3	2	1
2b.	Visions for improvement are always focused on students, teaching, and learning.		Visions for improvement are sometimes focused on students, teaching, and learning.	Visions for improvement do not target students, teaching, and learning.	
2c.	Visions for improvement target high-quality learning experiences for all students.		Visions for improvement address quality learning experiences in terms of students' abilities.	Visions for improvement do not include concerns about the quality of learning experiences.	

3. The staff's collective learning and application of the learnings (taking action) create high intellectual learning tasks and solutions to address student needs.

	5	4	3	2	1
3a.	The entire staff meets to discuss issues, share information, and learn with and from one another.		Subgroups of the staff meet to discuss issues, share information, and learn with and from one another.	Individuals randomly discuss issues, share information, and learn with and from one another.	
3b.	The staff meets regularly and frequently on substantive student-centered educational issues.		The staff meets occasionally on substantive student-centered educational issues.	The staff never meets to consider substantive educational issues.	
3c.	The staff discusses the quality of their teaching and students' learning.		The staff does not often discuss their instructional practices nor its influence on student learning.	The staff basically discusses non-teaching and non-learning issues.	

(Continued)

	5	4	3	2	1
3d.	The staff, based on its learnings, makes and implements plans that address students' needs, more effective teaching, and more successful student learning.		The staff occasionally acts on its learnings and makes and implements plans to improve teaching and learning.	The staff does not act on its learning.	
3e.	The staff debriefs and assesses the impact of its actions and makes revisions.		The staff infrequently assesses its actions and seldom makes revisions based on the results.	The staff does not assess its work.	

4. Peers review and give feedback based on observing one another's classroom behaviors in order to increase individual and organizational capacity.

	5	4	3	2	1
4a.	Staff members regularly and frequently visit and observe one another's classroom teaching.		Staff members occasionally visit and observe one another's teaching.	Staff members never visit their peers' classrooms.	
4b.	Staff members provide feedback to one another about teaching and learning based on their classroom observations.		Staff members discuss non-teaching issues after classroom observations.	Staff members do not interact after classroom observations.	

5. School conditions and capacities support the staff's arrangement as a professional learning organization.

	5	4	3	2	1
5a.	Time is arranged and committed for whole staff interactions.		Time is arranged but frequently the staff fails to meet.	Staff cannot arrange time for interacting.	

	5	4	3	2	1
5b.	The size, structure, and arrangements of the school facilitate staff proximity and interaction.		Considering the size, structure, and arrangements of the school, the staff is working to maximize interaction.		The staff takes no action to manage the facility and personnel for interaction.
5c.	A variety of processes and procedures are used to encourage staff communication.		A single communication method exists and is sometimes used to share information.		Communication devices are not given attention.
5d.	Trust and openness characterize all of the staff members.		Some of the staff members are trusting and open.		Trust and openness do not exist among the staff members.
5e.	Caring, collaborative, and productive relationships exist among all staff members.		Caring and collaboration are inconsistently demonstrated among the staff members.		Staff members are isolated and work alone at their task.

LEARNING OPPORTUNITY 3.4

The Learning Community's WORK

To exist is to change, to change is to mature, to mature is to go on creating oneself endlessly.

—Henri Bergson

Outcome

Learners will identify and explain the structure of the work they do within the community. This explanation will include the steps they take for this work.

Assumption

The provision of expectations and structures to guide the organization's work significantly contributes to the clarity and specificity of the work and to realizing the goals of the end product.

Suggested Time

2 hours

Materials

- Flip chart and markers
- "Making the Promise a Reality" (see Resource A, p. 211)
- pp. 8–16, 19–20, and 144–145 of *Leading Professional Learning Communities: Voices From Research and Practice* (Hord & Sommers, 2008)

Learning Event

1. **Set the stage** by inviting participants to identify what they think the activities of the community of professional learners will be in their community meeting. Note these on the flip-chart pad without judging, assessing, or adding other commentary.

2. **Direct** learners to Hord and Sommers (2008), pp. 8–16 ("Characteristics of a Professional Learning Community"), reviewing briefly, and noting that one of these characteristics is the major focus of this session (collective learning and its application). Attention might be given to the last sentence in the first paragraph: "The PLC is not just about collaboration; it is collaborating to learn together about a topic the community deems important" (Hord & Sommers, 2008, p. 8).

   Also direct participants' attention to the last paragraph on p. 19 of Hord and Sommers (2008) and to the figure and the first paragraph on p. 20. These constitute a brief description of how to select the learning that is needed by the staff.

3. **Share** the material from "Making the Promise a Reality," asking learners to review the text on pages 112–113. In this section, the steps that the staff will take to identify the focus of its work are described. Ask the staff members to compare these steps with the suggestions made and recorded on the flip-chart paper. Discuss their responses across the group. Now, ask them to check those steps that they have experienced in their school improvement work. Typically, they will note that the professionals in the school have not been given the opportunity to determine what changes should be made in their teaching, and have not planned how they will learn to use the selected new content or new strategies. These activities are essential to the self-organizing PLC.

4. **Reinforce** the importance of these steps (identified in "Making the Promise a Reality") by sharing the material from Hord and Sommers (2008, pp. 144–145), and asking the community of learners to compare the steps in "Making the Promise a Reality" with the descriptions from Hord and Sommers (2008). At the conclusion, ask for questions or needs for clarification.

5. **Provide closure** by inviting participants to group with their grade-level teams or subject-matter academic teams and make plans for how the school's community can follow the steps (studied in the various papers) and apply them across the school. Groups should record their steps on flip-chart paper and hang the flip-chart paper on the walls. When they are posted, invite the participants to "parade" around the room, viewing flip charts (leaving one person from their team to answer questions that may arise from any of the viewers). After the "parade," the person who stayed with his or her team flip chart will present a 2-minute report to the whole group that reviews the small group plans. (These plans should be recorded cryptically on note paper.)

Future Application

After the session, the notes from the groups that were generated in this session's activities should be distributed to all groups. Groups will meet to review all plans and identify commonalities of the reports. These notes will be the subject of focus in a near future session of the PLC, so that concrete plans may be made for the whole school's learning agenda.

Notes:

LEARNING OPPORTUNITY 3.5

Identifying a PLC Learning Goal

The idea of a school that can learn has become increasingly prominent during the last few years. It is becoming clear that schools can be re-created, made vital, and sustainably renewed not by fiat or command, and not by regulation, but by taking a learning orientation. This means involving everyone in the system in expressing their aspirations, building their awareness, and developing their capabilities together. In a school that learns, people who traditionally may have been suspicious of one another . . . recognize their common stake in the future of the school system and the things they can learn from one another.

—Senge, P. M., Cambron McCabe, N. H., Lucas, T., Kleiner, A., & Dutton, J.

Outcome

The members of the PLC will identify a learning goal to guide their work in learning together and ultimately to transfer their learning into affecting how students are learning.

Assumption

A PLC offers a significant staff development and school improvement approach that contributes to whole-school improvement and the school's overall effectiveness. Deliberate and carefully constructed learning for adults will produce better results for students.

Suggested Time

1–2 hours (or over a period of one to three PLC meetings)

Materials

- Flip chart and markers
- Student data that might be important to the PLC members
- "Identifying a Learning Goal for the PLC: Overview" (see p. 115; one copy for each participant)
- "Learning Focus Template" (see p. 117; one copy for each participant)

Learning Event

1. **Set the stage** by sharing the following quote with the PLC members. "We cannot emphasize enough that the major purpose of the PLC is the learning in which the adults in the school engage. When the professionals learn new practices, different instructional

strategies, and exciting curriculum, they become more effective with their students, and then students learn more successfully. Thus, an important aspect of the PLC is not only how well the PLC is functioning as an infrastructure or way of working, but how well the staff put into practice what they decided to learn, in order to serve students more effectively." (Hord & Sommers, 2008, p. 117).

You might have the quote printed out on 3 x 5 cards (one for each participant) and have each PLC member quietly journal on the back side what he or she believes the learning focus has been in the PLC during the past few months. Have each PLC member stand up and find someone who is not sitting next to him or her and exchange cards. They should go back to their seat and be prepared to share what was written on the card and why they think that has been the learning focus in the PLC.

On flip-chart paper, capture the *key* ideas identified as the learning going on in the PLC.

2. **Invite** PLC members to read, "Identifying a Learning Goal for the PLC: Overview." After reading, ask members to discuss the important reminders about the work of the PLC that were found in the overview. This might also be a good time to conduct an informal assessment around how the PLC has been doing its work, especially as it relates to intentional learning. You might create a T-chart and have the group identify the past successes of the PLC and its work and suggest what might be some areas to grow and stretch.

3. **Refer** to the flip chart that identified the focus areas for learning and ask the members what data were referenced to help reveal why these were important for the PLC to consider in its learning together. You might also discuss how many focus areas feel reasonable for the PLC to focus on when doing its learning work.

On another sheet of flip-chart paper, make a list of all data sources that the PLC should reference on a periodic basis to guide its consideration of where to focus its intentional learning in the future. Since data can wander in so many different directions, you might consider creating some groupings or headings that will help to collect data into meaningful focus areas or containers. Some examples might be the following: writing data, reading data, math data, and so on. It also helps to have various members assigned to help monitor, analyze, and report the data to the other PLC members during the year. If there is not a *clear* focus area for the PLC and its learning, suggest that members take the remaining time and locate and review important student learning data and prepare it to be reported out at the next meeting. They should use the "Learning Focus Template" to organize the data and communicate possible focus areas for the PLC to explore. It might be helpful to have members work in partners in the gathering of the student learning data.

4. **Guide** PLC members in using the "Learning Focus Template." There are three key areas for guiding the data-gathering process to help determine where the PLC should focus its learning. Part 1 involves identifying specific indicators relating to student achievements that stand out as important. These indicators can be areas to celebrate as well as areas that need improvement. The student data indicator should include the source of data and the performance level for student learning. For example, "**SAT**: Our SAT scores improved 50 points in the last year but have consistently fluctuated above and then below the 1000-point mark."

You can have as many indicators that you feel are necessary to tell the data story for how students are achieving in the school. You can use the backside of the template to record your data indicators. Try to keep all your indicators focused around one of the groupings or headers for student learning.

Part 2 requires making a list of questions that should be asked or explored within the PLC around these indicators. For example, in the data around SAT scores, you might ask, "What might be creating the fluctuations in student scores? What parts of the curriculum that we teach directly impacts how students might perform on the SAT?" Try to identify as many questions as you can.

Part 3 uses the questions to identify a possible learning focus for the PLC to explore in its learning work together. The learning goal should be structured as a large banner question to help guide the PLC's learning. For example, "How do curriculum, classroom assessment, and course offerings affect the level of success students might have on the SAT?"

5. **Provide closure** by having data partners report out and share their "Learning Focus Template" at the next meeting. The PLC can then use the templates to determine one or two learning focus areas that the PLC has the most energy and commitment to explore in its learning and then transfer into classroom practice.

Future Application

PLC members should keep the "Learning Focus Templates" that are not the current priority of the learning work for future consideration. It is also suggested that PLC agendas clearly articulate what the learning focus area is for the work. You might keep track of how much time during PLC meetings is spent on logistics and how much time is spent in learning together through inquiry, shared best practices, action research, and the sharing of research or scholarly articles.

Notes:

IDENTIFYING A LEARNING GOAL FOR THE PLC: OVERVIEW

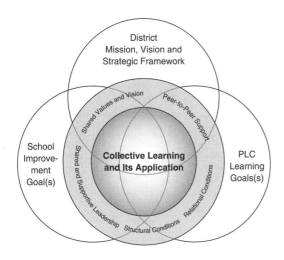

Members of a PLC are expected to recognize that their learning will be the key to their students' learning.

Members of the PLC are expected to acknowledge their own learning needs in their quest to support their students' success.

Their true purpose must be improved staff and student performance – Thus, the consistent guiding purpose of the PLC is student learning success.

Because all change and improvement is dependent on learning, the professional learning community is a structure and way of working that provides the environment in which principals and teachers set about intentionally learning in order to increase their effectiveness and increase student results.

The PLC should be considered as three dimensional: One dimension is the encompassing shell that provides the structure within which the second dimension of the PLC takes place—that is, the work of the PLC. The structural shell includes the following components:

- The shared values and vision of the participants that guide their work
- The development of shared and supported leadership that involves everyone in decision making about the work of the PLC
- The structural or physical or logistical conditions that support the operations of the PLC
- The relational conditions—the human attitudes and perspectives, and the regard that the members share with each other
- The peer-to-peer support that members give to each other as they observe each other at work and provide feedback

The inner shell is the collective learning that contributes unceasingly to quality teaching and student learning.

It is here that the staff initiates its work through the examination of a wide array of student performance data to assess the productivity of their teaching, and how those data also indicate the students' needs.

The third dimension aligns the learning in the PLC with the district's mission, vision, and strategic framework as well as the school's improvement goal(s). These all work together in harmony to increase the chances for all students to be successful in their learning.

The PLC members begin by identifying a learning goal that will focus on their purpose for coming together to learn and then later applying that learning into making a difference for their students. To find their learning goal the PLC uses the following steps:

1. The PLC reflects on its work for students and related student outcomes as indicated from the data. They evaluate the extent to which their practices and programs are producing the results that they intended.

2. The PLC determines how well the students are being served (where the staff is succeeding with students' high-quality learning and where it is not so successful) through the study of the data.

3. The PLC identifies student achievement areas in need of attention.

4. Because multiple student needs cannot be addressed simultaneously, the staff also specifies priority areas and determines from the data those in need of immediate attention.

5. The PLC engages in studying solutions for the needed areas in order to make decisions about the adoption of new practices or programs. As the staff members broadly explore the most relevant and powerful means for addressing students' needs, they may well require professional learning in order to learn about and develop robust criteria for use in selecting new approaches or programs to use in their classrooms.

Notes:

Adapted from Hord, S. M., & Sommers, W.A. *Leading Professional Learning Communities: Voices from Research and Practice.* Copyright © 2008 Corwin Press. A joint publication of Corwin Press and the National Association of Secondary School Principals.

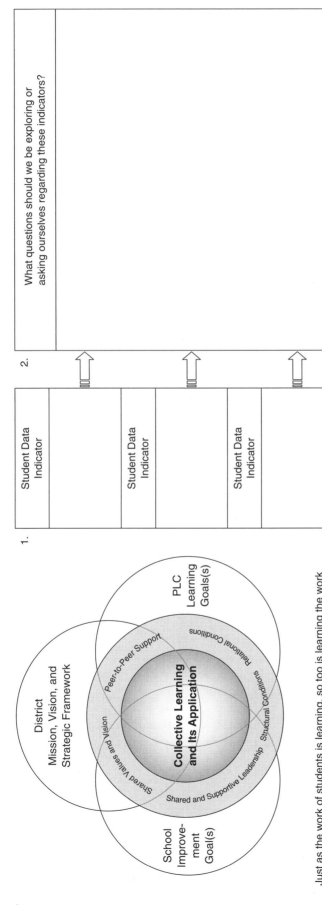

Just as the work of students is learning, so too is learning the work of the professional learning community. Knowledge and learning are socially constructed and are most fruitfully produced in a social setting with others. The professional learning community offers a structure that accelerates and supports the professional learning of the adults in the school in a community setting. Thus, a professional learning community offers a significant staff development and school improvement approach that contributes to whole-school improvement and the school's overall effectiveness. Hord and Hirsh, Making the Promise a Reality

2. What questions should we be exploring or asking ourselves regarding these indicators?

1.

Student Data Indicator	
Student Data Indicator	
Student Data Indicator	
Student Data Indicator	

3. Our PLC Learning Goal:

LEARNING OPPORTUNITY 3.6

Traffic Light Indicator

As we learn more about who we are, we can learn techniques that reveal rather than conceal the personhood from which good teaching comes.

—Parker Palmer

Outcome

Learners will describe their current state of openness to learning. The goal is to be aware of your own state of mind regarding learning.

Assumption

Schools are busy places with many demands. Staff members are not always in the best state of mind to be in a learning situation. That is part of life. If we are not aware of our frame of mind, we may make assumptions that get in the way of our own learning.

This learning opportunity is to provide a nonjudgmental way of assessing whether or not we are in an optimal learning state. This awareness can help us try to shift into a more productive state and allow us to ask others for help during the learning opportunity.

Sometimes using a metaphor such as the traffic light for learning can facilitate conversations that otherwise may be too difficult.

Suggested Time

1 hour

Materials

- Flip chart and markers
- "The Traffic Light Indicator" (see p. 120; one copy for each participant)

Learning Event

1. **Set the stage** by asking participants to read the "Traffic Light Indicator."

2. **Invite** participants to use the descriptions of the "Traffic Light Indicator" material to assess and share in which "light" each person currently resides. Make sure everyone has a chance to speak.

3. **Ask** participants, "What would help you move toward the green light or assist you in remaining at the green light during the PLC session?" Record these ideas on flip-chart paper.

4. **Reflect** on the past week. Which light has been dominant? What factors have been present that have caused this light position? Chart the factors.

5. **Consider** the last month or the school year, and ask participants, "What has contributed to your traffic light indicator? What are some ways you have been able to move from red or yellow toward green?" Record these ideas on the flip chart, and rate each as having either a strong potential for supporting movement, having modest potential, or having a disappointing impact.

6. **Develop** a list of the strategies people have found to be most helpful. What can the PLC group do that would support each participant's learning? Solicit suggestions from the group.

7. **Provide closure** by asking "What are some helpful hints that the PLC group wants to remember for individuals and the group when a yellow or red light appears?" Make a list in a learning journal or in notes of the meeting.

Future Application

Think about what other applications of the "Traffic Light Indicator" could be used for committees or groups in which you are a member. What are possible applications of this learning opportunity in classrooms?

Notes:

THE TRAFFIC LIGHT INDICATOR

You can monitor yourself in a PLC through the use of a simple traffic light indicator. The traffic light becomes an intention that holds the best possibility for how you choose to show up and be fully present in your PLC. The traffic light is not about being wrong or right. It is simply noticing yourself and your interactions with others in a learning community.

Red

I choose to withhold my ideas or I may look to someone else as the expert to further the thinking in the group. When a problem is surfaced in the PLC, I immediately start looking for a silver bullet or a quick fix. I spend my time thinking how this PLC is being mandated from the administration and I have other kinds of work I want to be doing right now.

Yellow

I participate in parking lot conversations on topics related to our PLC. I show up having the "right" answer and speak with authority about what I know is the right thing to do. When an innovative or compelling idea is presented, I immediately move the group back to the practical tasks at hand.

Green

I embrace all ideas presented in the PLC with curiosity and wonderment. I find myself interested in how others think and see the world around them. I find a balance between advocacy and inquiry when expressing myself in a PLC. I notice when I get hooked to an idea or belief and pause long enough to determine if that hook is helpful to others and me. I actively interrogate reality. I use learning in the group to see others and myself in order to be more effective in my work.

Notes:

Component 4

Relational Conditions

OVERVIEW AND CURRENT THINKING

Relational factors support the learning community's human and interpersonal development of openness, truth telling, and attitudes of respect and high regard for each of the members. In a true PLC, open dialogue, discussion, and debate occur regularly, with all members sharing in the celebrations of successful goal achievement.

It is not hard to understand and to acknowledge the imperative of trust among the members of the PLC. Numerous researchers have found this variable to be one of the most important factors in school improvement and establishing PLCs. PLC members frequently cite its absence as a barrier to productive relationships and to collaborative participation. How else can empathetic listening, open conversation, and transparent discussion occur? Individuals must believe that if they contribute a less-than-popular perspective, they won't be chastised or frowned upon. Conflicting views (attended by conflict resolution strategies) give variety and richness to the interactions of the community. Positive trust is vital to the staff's giving and receiving feedback.

Most PLC members express and demonstrate positive attitudes toward schooling, students, and other members. Contributing to positive relationships are the staff's clear focus on continuous learning and their norms of critical inquiry and culture of ongoing improvement. These collegial relationships support the staff's risk taking, its sense of efficacy toward effecting change, and its ownership of both challenging issues and their solutions.

LEARNING OPPORTUNITY 4.1

The Importance of Trust in the PLC

Trust is a human virtue, cultivated through speech, conversation, commitments, and action.

—Solomon & Flores (2001)

Outcome

PLC members will articulate the five facets of trust that can affect the ways they interact. Each member will identify specific behaviors that he or she can express to build, nurture, and sustain trusting relationships in the PLC.

Assumption

Trust is the social lubricant that allows humans to work together in respectful and transparent ways. When adults don't trust each other, they limit their potential for impacting student learning and success.

Suggested Time

1–1.5 hours

Materials

- Flip chart and markers
- "Relational Factors, Human Capacities, and the Importance of Trust in the PLC" (see p. 125; one copy for each participant)
- "Five Facets of Trust for Building, Nurturing, and Sustaining PLC Relationships" (see p. 126; one copy for each participant)
- "Action Steps for Building Trust" (see p. 127; one copy for each participant and one enlarged copy, viewable by the group, on a flip chart to use in Step 4 of the learning event)

Learning Event

1. **Set the stage** by asking PLC members to describe what they know about themselves when they are in a highly trusting relationship. In what ways are they able to express themselves differently in a relationship where there is a lot of trust versus in a relationship where there is little trust? You might post these on flip-chart paper in a T-chart format.

2. **Give** each member a copy of "Relational Factors, Human Capacities, and the Importance of Trust in the PLC."

Ask members to read the quote at the top of "Relational Factors, Human Capacities, and the Importance of Trust in the PLC": "Without the confidence that a person's words can be relied upon and can accurately predict future actions, trust is unlikely to develop" (Tschannen-Moran, 2004, p. 22). Ask members what they have noticed about the importance of trust in their work with colleagues in the years they have been teaching. How do trusting relationships make a difference for students and their learning?

Invite PLC members to find a learning partner with whom they can process the one-page overview within a "Say Something" activity. Once they have a partner, ask them to read quietly one paragraph at a time. After reading each paragraph, they should turn to one another and say *one* thing to their learning partner that the reading provoked in their thinking or reflecting.

At the end of the "Say Something" activity, ask PLC members to identify one thing they don't want to forget regarding trust and the PLC.

3. **Distribute** "Five Facets of Trust for Building, Nurturing, and Sustaining PLC Relationships." Assign each member one of the five facets of trust. If there are enough PLC members, have those who are assigned the same facet work together. Ask the members to read their facet in the chart and then discuss any additional understandings they may hold about that particular facet of trust.

   Next, give each group a piece of flip-chart paper (there should be five groups for the five facets) and ask them to write three things:

   • A definition of their facet that would be easy for other members in the PLC to understand

   • A symbol that could represent that facet of trust

   • One example for how that facet could be expressed as a human behavior in the PLC

   When the groups have finished charting, ask them to report to the other PLC members what they have charted and discussed.

4. **Guide** members back to "Five Facets of Trust for Building, Nurturing, and Sustaining Relationships." Ask members to rank from 1 to 5 (1 is most important, 5 is least important) the facets that matter most to him or her in the PLC. They can write their numbers inside the arrow extending out from each facet. When they have finished prioritizing the five facets of trust, chart the totals on the enlarged copy of "Action Steps for Building Trust."

   Ask for a show of hands for those who ranked each facet as number 1. Start with Honesty and work your way down the chart. If ten people chose Honesty as number 1, then write the number 10 in the box where it says Honesty. When you have completed the totals for each facet, you will have a composite of the facets that are of highest priority to PLC members.

5. **Provide closure** by identifying specific behaviors you most want to acknowledge and support in the PLC in order to build and nurture trust. To do this, the group will add information in the two columns: *Why is this facet of trust important to our work?* and *What behaviors can be expressed to nurture this facet with others?*

We suggest you only focus on the two facets that were recognized as most important. You will want to start with an intention of why this facet is important in the learning work of PLC members. Once the group has agreed on the intention behind this facet, identify two or three behaviors that members could express to nurture and build this facet of trust in the PLC. For example, if reliability was chosen as most important, members might want to establish a behavior of *showing up to PLC meetings on time.* Another behavior might be, *if someone is given a task to accomplish for the group, it can be expected that it will be done.* These behaviors can then be posted in the room where members meet and can be referenced during future meetings.

Future Application

When the PLC is facing some kind of conflict, you might want to reference the five facets of trust. You should first check to see if members have been expressing the behaviors that most members found important. If that has been happening, then you will want to find out if something has changed in regard to a different facet of trust that is beginning to feel important to PLC members. Often, a conflict can emerge because one of the five facets that feels important is not being supported or acknowledged in the PLC.

Notes:

This learning opportunity was adapted by James L. Roussin, Generative Human Systems, from Megan Tschannen-Moran's work *Trust Matters: Leadership for Successful Schools* (2004).

Relational Factors, Human Capacities, and the Importance of Trust in the PLC

Without the confidence that a person's words can be relied upon and can accurately predict future actions, trust is unlikely to develop.

—Tschannen-Moran (2004)

Trust is the social lubricant that makes organizations run. When trust exists, organizations tend to think more creatively, take more risks, and share information more readily. There is a feeling of being supported. Wheatley (1996) declares that trust is the building block of an organization. Bryk and Schneider (2002) report how important relational trust is for schools. They studied 250 elementary schools in Chicago Public Schools after the district implemented a site-based management model in some schools. They looked at five variables: school governance, curriculum, teaching techniques, professional development, and trust. What they found was that if you corrected for school governance, curriculum, teaching techniques, or professional development, the result was a one in seven chance of positively affecting student achievement—not significant. When they corrected for trust, they found a one in two chance of positively affecting student achievement.

Think about it: when teachers trust other teachers, they share more, help each other, create more possibilities, and are supportive. We believe that is one of the outcomes important in schools and that PLCs promote and enhance those relationships.

Relationships in the PLC community should be based on mutual regard, respect, and caring. Attitudes are such that there is shared concern about all members of the professional community and the additional staff and students at the campus. The matter of relationships constitutes a significant variable of the culture, which is centered on the people and the human factors in the community.

These relationships are more positive and thus more powerful when they are characterized by reflection, porosity, and transparency. Think . . .

- mirrors for reflection,
- windows for transparency, and
- membranes for porosity.

That is, when the staff members in the school reflect individually and collectively about their work and its benefits for students, their work is more thoughtfully directed to desired student outcomes. When they interact with each other in an open and porous way, ideas can move more readily from one individual or grade level or department to others. When the spoken expressions and behaviors of the professionals are transparent and authentic, then trust can develop. Research has shown clearly that trust is a basic requirement for people in the school to work productively and pleasantly together (Bryk & Schneider, 2002). Reflection, porosity, and transparency contribute to the increase of the organization's flexibility and resilience.

Establishing trust will help to initiate conversations. A PLC requires trust to reach its full potential in making a difference for student learning.

Adapted from Hord, S. M., & Sommers, W. A. (2008). *Leading Professional Learning Communities*. Thousand Oaks, CA: Corwin Press.

FIVE FACETS OF TRUST FOR BUILDING, NURTURING, AND SUSTAINING PLC RELATIONSHIPS

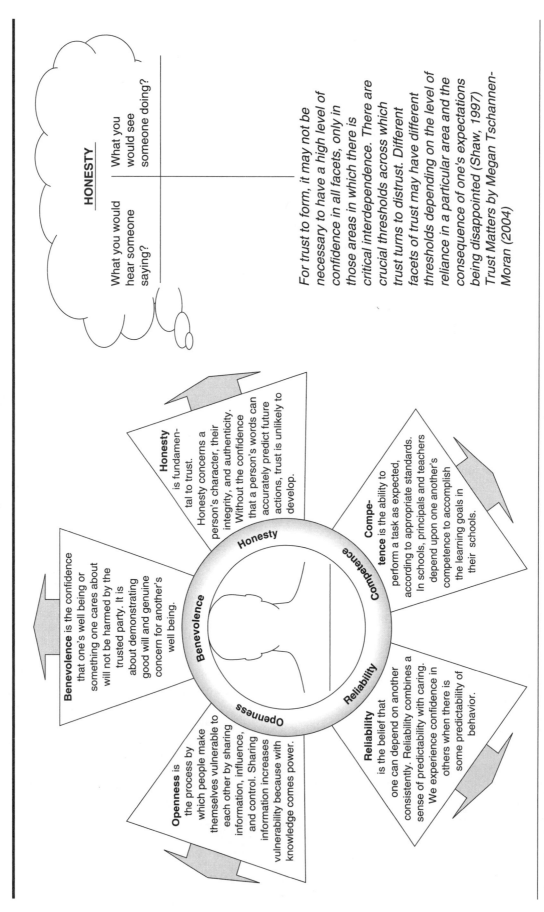

HONESTY

What you would hear someone saying?	What you would see someone doing?

For trust to form, it may not be necessary to have a high level of confidence in all facets, only in those areas in which there is critical interdependence. There are crucial thresholds across which trust turns to distrust. Different facets of trust may have different thresholds depending on the level of reliance in a particular area and the consequence of one's expectations being disappointed (Shaw, 1997) Trust Matters by Megan Tschannen-Moran (2004)

Honesty is fundamental to trust. Honesty concerns a person's character, their integrity, and authenticity. Without the confidence that a person's words can accurately predict future actions, trust is unlikely to develop.

Compe-tence is the ability to perform a task as expected, according to appropriate standards. In schools, principals and teachers depend upon one another's competence to accomplish the learning goals in their schools.

Benevolence is the confidence that one's well being or something one cares about will not be harmed by the trusted party. It is about demonstrating good will and genuine concern for another's well being.

Openness is the process by which people make themselves vulnerable to each other by sharing information, influence, and control. Sharing information increases vulnerability because with knowledge comes power.

Reliability is the belief that one can depend on another consistently. Reliability combines a sense of predictability with caring. We experience confidence in others when there is some predictability of behavior.

Honesty
Competence
Benevolence
Openness
Reliability

Adapted from Tschannen-Moran. M. (2004). *Trust Matters: Leadership for Successful Schools.* San Francisco, CA: Jossey Bass.

ACTION STEPS FOR BUILDING TRUST

Trust Facet	Why is this facet of trust important to our work?	What behaviors can be expressed to nurture this facet with others?
Honesty		
Competence		
Reliability		
Openness		
Benevolence		

LEARNING OPPORTUNITY 4.2

Group Development

The winners of the future will be those who can build teams and build people.

—Thomas Harvey and Bonita Drolet

Outcome

Learners will identify the stages of group formation, determine where the PLC group currently exists, and implement plans for the group to move toward the performing stage.

Assumption

Group formation is not easy and takes time to develop common purpose and norms to function well. Bruce Tuckman's model has served as a guide for many years and in many circumstances.

Suggested Time

1 to 1.5 hours

Materials

- Flip chart and markers
- "Stages of Group Development" (see p. 130; one copy for each participant) or download and/or electronically distribute "Tuckman's Stages Model" (forming, storming, norming, and performing) from http://en.wikipedia.org/wiki/Group_development#Tuckman .27s_Stages_model OR http://www.businessballs.com/tuckmanformingstormingnorming performing.htm

Learning Event

1. **Set the stage**: Read "Stages of Group Development" or the downloaded article.

2. **Invite** participants to state which stage they believe the group is currently in and specific reasons to support their view. Make sure everyone has a chance to speak.

3. **Describe** processes or behaviors that will strengthen the current stage of development and help to transition to the next stage.

4. **Ask** participants to identify the next stage and specify what individual and group behaviors they would see and hear that would be an indicator of the next stage.

5. **Provide closure** by using the flip chart and markers to record the examples, behaviors, or norms of the next stage for reference at future meetings. Send a list of those examples, behaviors, or norms to all participants after the meeting.

Future Application

After four to six additional meetings, review the examples, behaviors, or norms agreed upon. What is the group doing that is like the stage of group development they want to be? What is the group doing that is different from what is desired? How can the group be more congruent with the desired behaviors?

Notes:

STAGES OF GROUP DEVELOPMENT

The Forming—Storming—Norming—Performing model of group development was first proposed by Bruce Tuckman in 1965, who maintained that these phases are all necessary and inevitable in order for the team to grow, to face up to challenges, to tackle problems, to find solutions, to plan work, and to deliver results.

Forming

In the first stages of team building, the *forming* of the team takes place. The team meets and learns about the opportunity and challenges, and then agrees on goals and begins to tackle the tasks. Team members tend to behave quite independently. They may be motivated but are usually relatively uninformed of the issues and objectives of the team. Team members are usually on their best behavior but very focused on themselves. Mature team members begin to model appropriate behavior even at this early phase. Sharing the knowledge of the concept of "Teams: Forming, Storming, Norming, and Performing" is extremely helpful to the team.

Supervisors of the team tend to need to be directive during this phase. The forming stage of any team is important because in this stage the members of the team get to know one another, exchange some personal information, and make new friends. This is also a good opportunity to see how each member of the team works as an individual and how they respond to pressure.

Storming

Every group enters the *storming* stage in which different ideas compete for consideration. The team addresses issues such as what problems they are really supposed to solve, how they will function independently and together, and what leadership model they will accept. Team members open up to each other and confront each other's ideas and perspectives. In some cases, *storming* can be resolved quickly. In others, the team never leaves this stage. The maturity of some team members usually determines whether the team will ever move out of this stage. Some team members will focus on minutiae to evade real issues.

The *storming* stage is necessary to the growth of the team. It can be contentious, unpleasant, and even painful to members of the team who are averse to conflict. Tolerance of each team member and their differences needs to be emphasized. Without tolerance and patience the team will fail. This phase can become destructive to the team and will lower motivation if allowed to get out of control.

Supervisors of the team during this phase may be more accessible but tend to still need to be directive in their guidance of decision-making and professional behavior. The groups will therefore resolve their differences and group members will be able to participate with one another more comfortably and they won't feel that they are being judged in any way and will therefore share their own opinions and views.

Norming

At some point, the team may enter the *norming* stage. Team members adjust their behavior to each other as they develop work habits that make teamwork seem more natural and fluid. Team members often work through this stage by agreeing on rules, values, professional behavior, shared methods, working tools, and even taboos. During this phase, team members begin to trust each other. Motivation increases as the team gets more acquainted with the project.

Teams in this phase may lose their creativity if the norming behaviors become too strong and begin to stifle healthy dissent and the team begins to exhibit groupthink.

Supervisors of the team during this phase tend to be participative more than in the earlier stages. The team members can be expected to take more responsibility for making decisions and for their professional behavior. As team members get to know each other better, their views of each other begin to change. The team feels a sense of achievement for getting so far, however some members can begin to feel threatened by the amount of responsibility they have been given. They would try to resist the pressure and revert to storming again.

Performing

Some teams will reach the *performing* stage. These high-performing teams are able to function as a unit as they find ways to get the job done smoothly and effectively without inappropriate conflict or the need for external supervision. Team members have become interdependent. By this time they are motivated and knowledgeable. The team members are now competent, autonomous, and able to handle the decision-making process without supervision. Dissent is expected and allowed as long as it is channeled through means acceptable to the team.

Supervisors of the team during this phase are almost always participative. The team will make most of the necessary decisions. Even the most high-performing teams will revert to earlier stages in certain circumstances. Many long-standing teams will go through these cycles many times as they react to changing circumstances. For example, a change in leadership may cause the team to revert to *storming* as the new people challenge the existing norms and dynamics of the team.

Notes:

LEARNING OPPORTUNITY 4.3

Mapping Collaborative Interactions

The interactions between formal and informal leaders are indicative of collaboration and a focus on learning. The strength of the interactions between the leaders and the followers are also primary in sustaining professional learning communities. Time and energy must be spent on monitoring and strengthening those interactions.

—Hord & Sommers (2008)

Outcome

The PLC will monitor and calibrate their communications around seven norms of collaboration.

Assumption

The ways we interact affect how we learn together and ultimately how we transfer our learning into making a difference for our students. The better our interactions are, the more likely it is that our working together will produce significant results.

Suggested Time

45–90 minutes

Materials

- "Collaborative Culture" (see p. 134; one copy for each participant)
- "Mapping Collaborative Interactions: Instruction Guide" (see p. 138; one copy for each participant)
- "Template: Mapping Collaborative Interactions (MCI) Through Seven Norms" (see p. 140; one copy for each participant)

Learning Event

1. **Set the stage** by inviting PLC members to read "Collaborative Culture."

2. **Ask** the members to identify the key ideas in the article and to discuss (in their table groups, or across the large group) why the ideas are important to the work of the PLC.

3. **Invite** PLC members to read "Mapping Collaborative Interactions: Instruction Guide."

4. Referring to "Mapping Collaborative Interactions: Instruction Guide," walk the PLC through the template, taking the four-implementation steps one at a time.

5. **Provide closure** by reviewing everyone's norm and asking how they will remember their norm when the PLC returns for future meetings.

Future Application

At a future PLC meeting, consider having one of the members serve as a process observer for one of the seven norms. He or she can then report how successful the group was in manifesting that norm during the meeting.

Notes:

COLLABORATIVE CULTURE

Robert J. Garmston

Right Way to Begin Depends on Where You Are Right Now

Sally Oxenberry was asked to facilitate the leadership team that meets weekly at her middle school and to help develop a spirit of collaboration. The school staff is organized into teams of five or six people. Oxenberry works with the team leader. She had modeled collaborative practices such as paraphrasing but didn't know what other skills to teach and in what sequence.

"It's all such good stuff, but where do I begin?" she asked (personal communication, 2006). "I feel that we need to do dialogue and ways of talking before going any further; however, I also feel we can learn so much from the seven norms of collaboration."

> In this column, I will explore how attention to creating a collaborative culture can improve curriculum and student learning. Curriculum, as used here, is meant to convey the system, which addresses what is taught, how it is taught, and the mechanisms by which it is assessed.

The overarching rationale for changing the work culture to become more collaborative is culture's impact on learning. By melding an understanding that culture affects learning with a research-based vision of ways faculties interact to improve student learning, leaders can make a significant impact on achievement. In this column, I will explore how attention to creating a collaborative culture can improve curriculum and student learning. Curriculum, as used here, is meant to convey the system, which addresses what is taught, how it is taught, and the mechanisms by which it is assessed.

Oxenberry's dilemma is common. No one right way exists to develop collaborative cultures capable of improving student learning. Leaders start with rationale, or successful experiences of authentic dialogue, or introduce communication skills and structures for inquiry. Where to begin depends on context, understanding the dynamics of the group, and intuition, but all require leadership.

Leadership

Leaders who learn publicly are continuing inquirers, confident enough that they can reveal their own thinking in progress, are genuinely curious, and are provocateurs of collaborative cultures. They successfully promote high expectations, a spirit of inquiry, and an unwavering focus on learning for both students and adults.

In one urban system in which I work, the associate superintendent tells groups, "We are failing our kids." This reason and test data are the motivators she offers to groups to continuously develop capacities for collaboration focused on learning. She knows that to affect student learning, groups must "engage in structured, sustained, and supported instructional discussions that investigate the relationships between instructional practices and student work" (Supovitz & Christman, 2003).

Leaders at all levels—principals, department heads, grade level leaders, and others—can develop the communication capacities necessary to function as professional learning communities. They provide time and space for groups to meet and talk, encourage talk about substantive topics related to learning, and introduce protocols that make it safe to talk about difficult-to-discuss topics and skills.

One Way to Start

One place to begin to develop communication skills needed for effective collaboration is with the seven norms of collaboration (Garmston & Wellman, 2009).

Norms are important because they are the foundation tools with which groups can dialogue, engage productively in conflict, discuss and decide, invent and problem solve. Each time I have observed a member of a group, a grade-level team, a department, or an advisory group paraphrase spontaneously, I have witnessed a watershed experience that makes all further conversations more efficient and effective.

Taken at face value, these norms seem simple and perhaps not worthy of faculty attention. Most adults believe they know most of these skills. But there is an enormous difference between declaring one knows how to use a skill and skillfully, habitually using the skill in work conversations. These seven practices are skills that transform to norms when they become habits in a group. Norms signal expected behavior. Two payoffs occur when a practice becomes a norm: Because members are conscious of the behavior, they voluntarily monitor both themselves individually and the group; and norms inform and shape the behaviors of new members. The seven norms of collaboration are:

Promote a spirit of inquiry: Learning is, at its root, a questioning process. True collaboration requires questioning one's own and others' thinking.

Pause: Pausing before responding or asking a question allows group members time to think and enhances dialogue, and discussion, and decision making.

Paraphrase: Using a paraphrase starter that is comfortable for you—"So ..." or "As you are ..." or "You're thinking ..."—and following the starter with a paraphrase helps members of the group hear and understand each other as they formulate decisions.

Probe: Using gentle open ended probes or inquiries such as "Please say more ..." or "I'm curious about..." increases the clarity and precision of the group's thinking.

Put ideas on the table: Ideas are the heart of a meaningful dialogue. Label the intention of your comments. For example, you might say, "Here is one idea ..." or "One thought I have is . . . " or "Here is a possible approach ..."

Pay attention to oneself and others: Meaningful dialogue is facilitated when each group member is conscious of himself or herself and of others and is aware of not only what he or she is saying, but also how it is said and how others are responding. This includes paying attention to learning style when planning for, facilitating, and participating in group meetings. Responding to others in their own language forms is one manifestation of this norm.

Presume positive intentions: Assuming that others' intentions are positive promotes and facilitates meaningful dialogue and eliminates unintentional put downs. Verbalizing supposed positive intentions is one manifestation of this norm.

Self-assessment

After introducing the norms, use self-assessment inventories, such as the one above, to monitor meetings and enroll group members to learn and apply the norms. Additional detailed inventories can he found at www.adaptiveschools.com/sevennorms.htm. These inventories help with introducing norms and determining which to work on first. For example, one inventory focuses on "me," the degree to which I put ideas on the table and so on. Another assesses "we," the degree to which the group puts ideas on the table and so on.

To select a common norm to focus on, assign one "we" inventory to groups of four to assess the behaviors of the entire group. Gather the results and display the data so the full group can see each subgroup's ratings. Next, facilitate a conversation about the results: "Help us understand what you were paying attention to that generated a rating of 2 on that norm." This talk brings to the surface what already exists. The first step in improvement is awareness.

Engage the group in describing what that norm would look and sound like in meetings. Then monitor the use of the norm frequently, because what is inspected is expected. "How are we doing on our norm during this meeting? What might we want to acknowledge, and what might we want to pay more attention to?"

Norms of collaboration:

Assessing consistency in a group at key work setting

1. Promoting a spirit of inquiry

Low • ————————————————— • High

2. Pausing

Low • ————————————————— • High

3. Paraphrasing

Low • ————————————————— • High

4. Probing

Low • ————————————————— • High

5. Putting ideas on the table and pulling them off

Low • ————————————————— • High

6. Paying attention to self and others

Low • ————————————————— • High

7. Presuming positive intentions

Low • ————————————————— • High

Ad hoc groups will sometimes invite members to suggest "group norms." While this practice can be helpful, there are distinctions between these types of norms and the seven norms of collaboration. Group generated norms most often are conceptual, such as a norm requesting "respectful listening" or "freedom from attack." They are easy to agree to, but it is difficult to ascertain whether the norm is being followed. I refer to these as "behavior agreements." The seven norms, for the most part, are stated behaviorally, but are more precise and can be monitored.

Develop the norms of collaboration for more than meetings. These norms are useful to spread throughout all the conversations in the school. As collaboration in conversation develops, a collaborative culture begins to form. And culture affects learning.

References

Garmston, R., & Wellman, B. (2009). *The adaptive school: A sourcebook for developing collaborative groups.* Norwood, MA: Christopher Gordon.

Supovitz, J., & Christman, J. B. (2003, November). *Developing communities of instructional practice: Lessons from Cincinnati and Philadelphia.* (CPRE Policy Briefs RB-39). Philadelphia, PA: University of Pennsylvania, Graduate School of Education.

Notes:

MAPPING COLLABORATIVE INTERACTIONS

Instruction Guide

A major tension is that all groups have more tasks to accomplish than time in which to accomplish them. Yet any group that is too busy to reflect on process is too busy to improve.

–Garmston & Wellman (2009)

Garmston and Wellman (2009) have identified a set of norms that invite seven specific moves for effective group interaction. These moves are called the Seven Norms of Collaboration and include (1) Promoting a Spirit of Inquiry, (2) Pausing, (3) Paraphrasing, (4) Probing, (5) Placing Ideas on the Table, (6) Paying Attention to Self and Others, and (7) Presuming Positive Intentions. PLC collaboration will be more effective when group members monitor and calibrate for the seven norms while interacting.

We believe this can best happen when *one* of the norms is assigned to each group member. It then becomes that member's responsibility to mirror that norm for others in the group. By mirroring we mean to express that norm through observable behavior. This follows the thinking of psychologist Albert Bandura who believed that we could learn by observing others. He claimed that modeling has as much impact as direct experience.

"Mapping Collaborative Interactions" (MCI) is a tool to support the PLC facilitator in guiding the group to mirror the seven norms so they can be seen and hopefully mirrored back to one another. The MCI has four implementation steps: Intention, Definition, Listening, and Observable Behavior.

Steps 1 and 2—Intention and Definition Frame

Start by assigning one of the seven norms to each member of the group. The members will be responsible for actualizing their assigned norms for others when they are together. You will also want group members to keep their norms for at least a month so the potential for the norm to be embedded as a communication habit is greater.

The intention and definition frames work together. Have each group member read the definition for his or her norm. What lies behind the definition is an intention. That intention is the foundation for monitoring and expressing the norm. Merriam-Webster's dictionary defines intention as "a determination to act in a certain way." When you have a clear intention, it engages your attention. After participants have read their definitions, have each write an intention for his or her assigned norm in the space provided. There is no one right answer. The purpose is to find the intention that makes sense to each group member. As an example, a possible intention for putting inquiry at the center might be the following:

The intention behind putting inquiry at the center is to challenge our habituated ways of seeing, thinking, and acting. It is the reminder that a "certainty consciousness" limits the potential to be influenced by new or different ideas. By inviting inquiry, I am open to being influenced by the thinking of others and new ways of knowing. A spirit of inquiry helps us discover greater worlds of possibility for making a difference. (Author)

After everyone creates his or her intention, share aloud with the rest of the group before completing the listening frame. The intentions may invite a rich dialogue for how you want to work together in the PLC during the year.

Step 3—Listening Frame

Have each group member fill in the listening frame in order to identify how one would listen from that particular norm. For example:

> *I would listen from the norm of promoting a spirit of inquiry by hearing questions that invite the thinking of others; I would hear paraphrasing that acknowledges what others are saying. I would hear sentence stems like, "I wonder," "I am curious," "tell me more."*

The listening frame builds the capacity to monitor and calibrate a norm and then to identify when it is appropriate to mirror it back to the group.

Step 4—Observable Behaviors Frame

In their book *Influencer—The Power to Change Anything* (Patterson, Grenny, Maxfield, McMillan, Switzler, 2008), the authors identify what "master influencers" do to create change that lasts. A significant factor that they identified was the importance of envisioning a few vital behaviors related to the change you want to see. Once a person is able to SEE those few vital behaviors in his or her mind, the more capable the person is in expressing them.

If you want to make the norms "stick" for your group members, have them envision a few key behaviors that would be observed when their norm is being expressed. The more you are able to visualize a behavior the better able you are to express it. Have the group members then go back to their **MCI** form and capture the observable behavior that would be seen for their norm. When all the norms have been identified as behaviors, share them around the group and listen for common patterns of behavior that stretch across the norms.

References

Patterson, K., Grenny, J., Maxfield, D., McMillan, R., Switzler, A. (2008). *Influencer*. New York, NY: McGraw-Hill.

Bandura, A. (1977). *Social learning theory*. Englewood Cliffs, N.J.: Prentice-Hall.

Garmston, R. (Winter 2007). Collaborative culture, *Journal of Staff Development, 28*(1).

Garmston, R., & Wellman, B., (2009). *The adaptive school* (2nd ed.). Norwood, MA: Christopher-Gordon.

Notes:

Mapping Collaborative Interactions (MCI) Through Seven Norms

Intention	Norms of Collaboration	Listening Frame	Observable Behaviors
1.	**Putting Inquiry at the Center** Exploring perceptions, assumptions, beliefs, and interpretations promotes the development of understanding. Inquiring into the ideas of others before advocating for one's own ideas is important to productive dialogue and discussion.		• •
2.	**Pausing** Pausing before responding or asking a question allows time for thinking and enhances dialogue, discussion, and decision making.		• •
3.	**Paraphrasing** Using a paraphrase starter that is comfortable for you (such as "So . . . or "You're thinking . . .).		• •

Intention	Norms of Collaboration	Listening Frame	Observable Behaviors
4.	**Probing** Using gentle open-ended probes or inquiries (such as "Please say more about . . .").		• •
5.	**Placing Ideas on the Table** Ideas are the heart of meaningful dialogue and discussion. Label the intention of your comments. For example: "Here is one idea . . .").		• •
6.	**Paying Attention to Self and Others** Meaningful dialogue and discussion are facilitated when each group member is conscious of self and of others and is aware of what (s)he is saying and how it is said as well as how others are responding. This includes paying attention to learning styles when planning, facilitating, and participating in group meetings and conversations.		• •
7.	**Presuming Positive Intentions** Assuming that others' intentions are positive promotes and facilitates meaningful dialogue and discussion and prevents unintentional put-downs. Using positive intentions in speech is one manifestation of this norm.		• •

From *The Adaptive School: A Sourcebook for Developing Collaborative Groups*, 2nd edition, by Robert Garmston and Bruce Wellman. Norwood, MA: Christopher-Gordon, 2009. Used with permission.

LEARNING OPPORTUNITY 4.4

Relational Conditions

With facilitation, the ultimate control of the process is firmly in the hands of the participants, and the facilitator does not need to be an expert in the content of the issue.

—Straus (2002)

Outcome

PLC members will apply the understanding of four relational positions to their work.

Assumption

When we are interacting with others in a group, we usually move between asking questions and giving answers. The better we understand how we respond in a group, the more likely we can choose a mode of communication that can best serve the group's purpose and work.

Suggested Time

30–90 minutes

Materials

- "Four Relational Positions" (see p. 144; one copy for each participant)
- "Some Things PLCs DO!" (see p. 145; one copy for each participant)
- One set of circles from "Some Things PLCs DO!" cut out ahead of time and put in an envelope
- Scissors

Learning Event

1. **Set the stage** by giving PLC members "Four Relational Positions." The relational positions invite members to see four different ways they can interact when doing the work of the PLC.

2. **Invite** members to look at the line in the diagram identified as "ask questions, give answers."

3. **Ask** members in what situations would a PLC member be asking more questions than giving answers, and in what situations would a member choose to give more answers than questions?

4. **Explore** this question: how does a person determine when it is appropriate to give an answer and when it is appropriate to ask a question?

5. **Ask** members to discuss the situations when it is best to take the position of "self" as the expert, versus "other" as the expert. Ask also what the situations are where it might be best to see another as the expert and drawing out what they know.

6. **Place** the circles (that you have already cut out) in the envelope on the table so all members can see each circle. Each member will also have his or her own copy of "Some Things PLCs DO!"

7. **Ask** a PLC member to choose one of the circles that reveal *something a PLC does.* Have the member place the circle where it might be appropriate on the "Four Relational Positions" diagram. Then, ask him or her to talk out loud about which quadrant in *the four relational positions* might be the most appropriate for how members want to communicate around that particular activity of a PLC.

   There is *no one right answer* for this activity. The purpose is to help members become more sensitive in how they communicate in doing the work of a PLC.

   Another way you might use this activity is to have PLC members decide on the four most important things PLCs do and to decide where those four activities fit best on the diagram "Four Relational Positions."

   When all four activities are placed, have members create a story about what a PLC looks like when it is operating at its best doing those four activities.

8. **Provide closure** by asking each member how he or she will personally decide when to be in an "asking" mode and when to be in a "telling" mode. Also, ask how he or she will know when it is best to take the position of "self" as the expert, and when it is best to take the position of "other" as the expert.

Future Application

When the PLC seems to be unsure of its work, this activity might be helpful to assist members in thinking through where to focus time and effort so their collaboration is more productive. Use "Some Things PLCs DO!" and have members prioritize the activities from most important to least important. Have them select the top four ways they want to spend their time in a PLC. They can then take each one of those activities and identify action steps to support the work around each activity.

Notes:

FOUR RELATIONAL POSITIONS

Self as Expert

Ask Questions

Give Answers

Other as Expert

SOME THINGS PLCs DO!

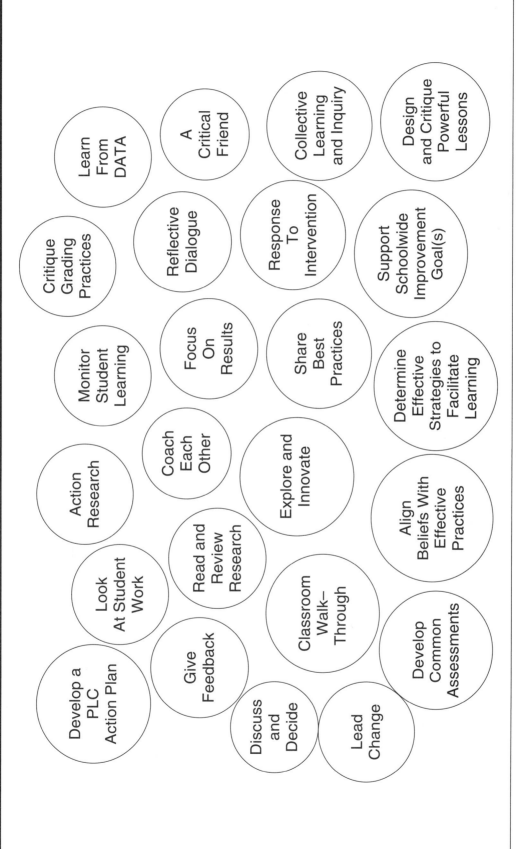

LEARNING OPPORTUNITY 4.5

Building Consensus

We did not all come over on the same ship, but we are all in the same boat.

—Bernard Baruch

Outcome

Participants will be able to diagnose conflict that may arise in their PLCs and manage the conflict to strengthen the PLC. The goal is *not* to stop conflict: the goal is to manage differing perspectives to make better decisions.

Assumption

PLCs, like most groups, have intelligent, committed people who do not necessarily think alike. The good news is different people bring different talents to the table. The bad news is thinking differently can cause conflict that stops the group from functioning at a high learning level.

Creative tension, differing ideas, and multiple perspectives can be the greatest strength for a group and its learning. If not managed appropriately, conflict can cause a rift in relationships and can reduce or stop learning. Many sources define conflict as a positive resource if managed correctly.

Suggested Time

60–90 minutes

Materials

- Flip chart and markers
- "Chadwick Process" (see p. 148; one copy for each participant)

Learning Event

1. **Set the stage** by inviting learners to identify the issues they believe are causing the conflict. Make sure everyone has a chance to speak. Everyone does not have to respond but everyone must have a chance to contribute. List these issues on the chart paper for future reference. Look at the list and ask, "Which one seems most pressing at this time?" Sometimes solving one issue will resolve other issues on the list.

2. **Ask** the participants, "What is the worst possible outcome if we do not manage this issue?" You do not have to chart this but it is important to get the fears out in the open.

Occasionally, ask, "What is the worst possible outcome if we *do* manage this issue?" These are the fears of what can happen in the future. Participants are worried about the future, based on the experience of the past, and having feelings in the present. Once all the concerns are expressed, move to the next question. Make sure you go in the opposite direction asking for responses. Do not start with the same person each round.

3. **Start** in the middle of the group going one direction and ask, "What is the best possible outcome for managing this issue?" Have a recorder chart the best possible outcomes. Write the words as they are spoken, but the recorder should not interpret what he or she thinks the participant is saying. *The best possible outcome is the goal of managing the conflict.*

4. **Optional**. You may not have time for this question or you may want to bypass it. However, professionals do not get a chance to talk about beliefs and values enough. Expressing their beliefs and values provides insight to what they think is important and why. Ask, "What beliefs and values are necessary in order for the best possible outcome to happen?" If you do this step, chart it.

5. **Start** in the middle of the group and, going the opposite direction from step 3, ask, "What strategies and actions are you willing to take in order to foster the best possible outcomes?" Chart the answers. You have the goals stated and charted. This question identifies actions professionals can take to realize the goal or goals. *This is your action plan.*

6. **Ask**, "What will be the evidence that we are getting closer to the best possible outcomes?" Chart the suggestions. *This is your assessment plan.* In the future, the group can see what progress will look like and determine whether or not the group is moving in that direction.

7. Make a summary of suggestions and send to the participants: (1) best possible outcomes, (2) strategies and actions, and (3) evidence of progress toward the best possible outcomes. Ask for feedback on the accuracy of your report.

8. **Decide** when to meet again to review progress. Without follow-up, there will be either backsliding or little progress. When professionals know there will be follow-up meetings to assess progress, more actions will take place.

9. **Provide closure** by reviewing the process. What is clearer now than before the process? What are the agreements made and who made them? What do we hope to see and hear as a result of this process?

10. **Optional.** When pressing issues come up or conflict continues over several meetings, it may be time to facilitate solutions using the Chadwick Process.

Future Application

In the group, determine if there are other issues that need to be addressed and whether or not this process will help gain clarity and build consensus. How might this process work with individual conflict? Other groups? In classrooms?

CHADWICK PROCESS

Bob Chadwick posits that conflict is generated over five basic issues: (1) change, (2) power, (3) scarcity, (4) diversity, and (5) civility. From our experience, this includes most of what we deal with in schools. Notice in the process it says, "manage conflict," not solve it. Sometimes we want creative solutions to build consensus rather than a situation where someone wins and someone loses.

Schools are in constant change. Think of the demographics, emerging brain research, new standards, and the list goes on. These issues cause change and discomfort. When we do not feel like we have any power in a situation, conflict and stress can result. Many decisions are being made outside the control of educators.

Scarcity is always a problem. There is never enough time or money to solve every societal problem. How do we handle diversity? People don't think alike (and we don't want them to). This isn't easy, but diverse opinions usually create positive solutions. If we cannot openly and honestly deal with differences of opinion, how will we be able to address gender, ethnicity, and all the other issues that divide us? Finally, civility: sometimes we don't treat each other very well.

St. Augustine said,

In essentials, we need unity.

In nonessentials, we need flexibility.

In everything, we need civility.

The process below can work for any of the five areas of conflict.

- Identify issues regarding the conflict (change, power, scarcity, diversity, civility).
- Ask, what is the worst possible outcome if we do not manage this issue?
- Ask, what are the best possible outcomes if we manage this issue?
- Ask, what are the beliefs and values necessary in order to foster the best possible outcomes?
- Ask, what strategies and actions are you willing to take to foster the best possible outcomes?
- Ask, what will be the evidence that we are moving toward the best possible outcomes?
- Ask, when will we meet again to assess progress toward our best possible outcomes?

Notes:

The authors learned this process from Bob Chadwick, Terrebonne, Oregon, in 1995.

LEARNING OPPORTUNITY 4.6

Defusing Conflict in a PLC

It is easier to stay out than get out.

—Chinese proverb

Outcome

PLC members will explain the "third point" facilitation method to reduce conflict and build consensus.

Assumption

In meetings, it is sometimes difficult to state an alternative viewpoint without evoking anger in another person, to advocate for a position without being pushy, or to be accused of being argumentative. When negative emotions get elevated, productivity usually decreases. When two people in a group get active, the rest of the group sometimes goes passive. There are ways to facilitate group activity to reduce one-to-one disagreements and focus on the overall goals of the PLC.

This learning opportunity can be used for presenting information (highly sensitive or difficult to hear), working with diverse opinions and viewpoints, or in an individual conversation. The term "third point" is used to identify the location of the information. Face-to-face conversation is with two people. The third point method involves two or more people and a third location, such as flip-chart paper, overhead, or whiteboard. The goal of this strategy is to have the group looking at and working with the third location rather than talking back and forth to one another. In this way, everyone is working to complete the graphic, written plan, or goal of the meeting using the "third point" rather than face-to-face conversations.

Suggested Time

1 to 1.5 hours

Materials

- Flip chart and markers
- A whiteboard, an overhead, or butcher paper

Learning Event

1. **Set the stage**: when conflict emerges during the PLC meeting, state the goal of the meeting and write it on the right side of the flip-chart paper.

2. **Ask** participants to identify any specific knowledge, skills, or applications of that goal, which will help clarify what the group will be seeing or hearing as a result of reaching that goal.

3. **Write** on the left side of the flip-chart paper the current situation. Include knowledge, skills, or applications that currently exist. Ask what strengths, problems, opportunities, and threats exist. Everyone in the room should be asked to contribute.

4. **Focus** on the third location (such as the flip-chart paper); it eases the tension between people. This reduces anxiety and frustration. When a person wants to challenge something, they speak to the flip-chart paper rather than to each other.

5. **Determine** the "how." Once the goal and description of that goal and its current state are visually represented, the group can concentrate on how to get from where they are to where they want to be. Chart this in between the goal and the current state. (Too many times we get mired in what's wrong—existing state—and never get clear about what we want.) Use this sequence, because the order is important.

6. **Check** accuracy and understanding. As a facilitator, once the goal, current state, and the how (actions) are written and visually recorded, do a final check to make sure everyone understands the intention and the required actions. Provide an opportunity for questions, clarifications, and alternatives.

7. **Provide closure** by debriefing the process. Did the group accomplish the task with less anxiety? Was developing a visual representation at a third location less threatening? Is there clarity of what the goal(s) and expectation(s) are in moving forward?

Future Application

Consider how this opportunity can be used in other situations where negative energy is anticipated. How might this be used in department or grade-level meetings? In district committee meetings? With individuals?

Notes:

Component 5

Intentional Collective Learning and Its Application

OVERVIEW AND CURRENT THINKING

So what is the purpose, the heart and soul, so to speak, of the PLC? Yes, the obvious answer is the learning that the professionals in the community deem useful to increase their effectiveness. Identifying the learning required of the staff is accomplished by a rigorous examination of multiple sources of student data to ascertain where they are performing successfully and where attention needs to be directed. Specifying desired new student outcomes provides the basis for determining what the administrators and teachers need to learn in order to achieve the new results with students.

To this end, the PLC conducts conversations targeted at students and their instructional needs and engages in reflective dialogue to assess their best course of action. Decisions are made collectively about *what* they will learn and *how* they will learn it. Furthermore, astute PLC members will determine upfront how they will monitor their progress in learning and in transferring their learning to the classroom. What occurs in the community does not stay in the community, but is meant to find its way into improved classroom practice. Thus, applying what is learned in the community's activities relies on effective implementation strategies, another challenge for many schools.

It is not sufficient that the professionals work together collaboratively on projects, although that is an important part of the agenda. It is true that learning may be a by-product of the collaborative, but is that learning what is needed by the staff to teach middle school students Algebra I tomorrow? Maybe, but maybe not. That is the explanation for beginning *deliberately* with what the staff needs to know and do, and then deciding how they will learn it.

Professionals, no matter in what field, are bound to a code of ethics, to a codified knowledge base, and to a commitment to the unceasing reference to and review of current research to identify new processes, procedures, technologies, strategies, content, and approaches. A very tall order! Thus, there is no time to "mess around" with what might be helpful, but might not. While we have schools so that students might have a supportive context in which to learn, the most significant factor in whether students learn well is teaching quality. Teaching quality is increased by continuous professional learning—the rationale for the creation and maintenance of the PLC.

LEARNING OPPORTUNITY 5.1

Leadership and the Enemies of Learning

Real learning gets to the heart of what it means to be human. Through learning we become able to do something we were never able to do before. Through learning we extend our capacity to create, to be part of the generative process of life.

—Senge (1993)

Outcome

This learning opportunity helps to set the conditions and possibly norms for deep learning to occur in the PLC.

Assumption

We often carry established "habits of learning" that may limit new learning from occurring or being open to information that feels different or unusual.

Suggested Time

1 hour

Materials

- Flip chart and markers
- Dots
- Highlighters
- "Leadership and the Enemies of Learning" (see p. 155; one copy for each participant)

Learning Event

1. **Set the stage** by asking each person in the PLC to reflect on and identify one behavior that supports new learning and one behavior that may get in the way of new learning. When everyone is ready, go around the group and share findings. You might chart these for later use in creating PLC learning norms.

2. **Share** "Leadership and the Enemies of Learning." While reading, each person should find at least two enemies of learning that might possibly show up in the PLC.

3. **Provide** 5–7 minutes so each person can create a learning principle for the two enemies of learning he or she identified in the reading. This learning principle will help the PLC

from being confronted by the enemies of learning. A learning principle might look like the following:

- o Enemy of Learning: Desire for clarity all the time.
- o Principle: Our PLC is open to allowing enough ambiguity to stir new thinking.

4. **Post** all the learning principles on flip-chart paper so everyone can see them.

5. **Identify** the four learning principles everyone agrees would be most helpful in supporting the PLC in its learning work. You can do this by giving each person four dots and ask them to place their dots on the four learning principles that would best guide PLC members in being powerful learners.

6. **Provide closure** by requesting each person in the PLC to adopt one of the four learning principles that he or she will model and mirror back to the whole group during the year in the PLC meetings.

Future Application

Present your learning principles on a large poster and add sticky notes where you typically meet. You also might add the learning principles to all your meeting agendas. You will want to periodically return to your learning principles to assess how the PLC is actualizing them in their work and learning together. Consider using the principles as a *check-out* at the end of each meeting to assess the PLC's learning capacity.

Notes:

LEADERSHIP AND THE ENEMIES OF LEARNING

One of the more interesting things about the current difficult economic environment has been watching how different business leaders have reacted to it. Those who have done the best to secure their companies' interests, protect their market positions, and retain their best people, have in my experience been those who immediately went into learning mode. Whether they look at the changes as an opportunity to learn new strategies for success, or simply to learn how to survive in the new environment, they have opened themselves and their organizations to learning. In doing so, they have discovered new possibilities for themselves and their companies.

That brings up the question, what sets a learner apart from those who are successful in one environment but cannot seem to find new actions that work in a different one? To answer that question it is important first to differentiate learning from simply amassing data. Learning creates a change in behavior, or at least the possibility for new behavior. It generates the potential to take new or different actions in the world.

Learning to ride a bicycle, for example, means being able to get on one and ride it when you want to. Before you couldn't, after you can. The same is true for learning new or different behaviors and actions in any other domain of life, including business [school] leadership, family, artistic expression, and community service. Learning opens us to new possibilities for action that may be more useful or appropriate for the context we find ourselves in. This is especially important when we suddenly find ourselves in a different context, such as a recession.

So, what makes it possible to learn new behaviors and actions quickly, or even to learn them at all? To put it simply, learners have eliminated almost all of their personal enemies of learning, those attitudes, emotions, and behavior patterns that dull or even kill our ability to learn.

Here are a few key enemies of learning, as described by Julio Olalla, the noted coach, writer and teacher:

> **Our inability to admit that we don't know**. We have learned the value of knowing and we devalue not knowing. But in order to learn we have to allow ourselves to be confused—to be able to say, "I don't know" without judging ourselves or others. "I don't know" is the place where new learning begins. When we say, "I already know that" we are limited to the assumptions we already have. Being able to say, "I don't know" without judgment is one of the great advantages children have which make them such fast learners. Olalla notes that "to be a child is to live in awe of the discovery of domains of action whose existence we were not capable of even anticipating."

Another powerful variation on this theme is the fear of admitting that we don't know. When knowing is so highly valued and not knowing devalued, I may assess that admitting I don't know something would cause others to devalue me. This can also prevent me from beginning the learning process.

- **The desire for clarity all of the time.** A prevailing attitude of many in our culture is wanting to be clear about everything all of the time. Like the inability to admit that we don't know, this deprives us of the process of inquiry.
- **Lack of priority for learning—"I don't have time."** One of the things we tell ourselves far too often in our super-fast-paced environment is, "The world is moving too fast and I don't have time to learn." We fail to consider that this is a problem of assigning

priorities—if we did we'd have to acknowledge our own responsibility. Learning must be a priority or it won't happen. The irony of a life that is so packed with doing that there is no time for learning is that little of value may ever actually get done. When what we are doing isn't working, simply doing the same things faster won't get us what we need and want. It is time to take time to learn new actions.

- **Inability to unlearn.** We assume that if it worked well before it should work well again. This is rarely so. For example, I used a DOS-based computer where I worked for some years. When I took a job at a new company where they used Macintosh computers I found that I had to unlearn what worked on a DOS computer in order to learn to use the Mac. Once I did so I became much more productive. But I couldn't have benefited from using the Mac unless I was willing to unlearn the DOS system. Imagine if I had continued to try typing "DIR" on my Mac screen every time I wanted to see my files! Yet many times we confront new situations by simply repeating old actions over and over again, frustrated that they don't work.

- **Ignoring the emotional dimension of learning.** Learning requires creation of the appropriate emotional field or context—one of respect and caring. Learning requires an opening to the new and a disposition to question what we already know. It also requires courage and trust. These form an emotional predisposition to learning without which it will not take place.

- **Ignoring the body as a dimension of learning.** We need to have a body that can house a new interpretation or perform a new action. New learning changes the body's physiology. Depending on what we learn, it may create changes in the neural structure of the brain, the electrochemistry of our nervous system, even the shape of the body. Whatever we do we do it with the body. The ability to learn requires the ability to open our bodies to change.

- **Confusing learning with acquiring information.** Far too often today we confound having lots of data with learning—if we "know" some new bit of information we consider that we have learned something. Yet simply possessing information doesn't give us a clue as to how to use it effectively. If we only have one or two possible interpretations for the data, neither of which seem to get us where we want to go, we will have to learn a new interpretation. Learning has to do with effective action.

- **Not giving permission to others to teach us.** When we declare someone to be our teacher we invest him or her with trust and authority. We recognize that they are more effective in a particular domain of action than we are and we declare that we want to be more effective in that domain than we currently are. When we do not give a teacher permission to teach us, we rob ourselves of the opportunity to learn. There are many ways in which we deny this permission. We may fear admitting to a potential teacher that we don't know. Conversely, we may believe that we know as much as—or more than—he or she does. We may believe we can—or should—learn whatever it is by ourselves. We may believe we are incapable of being taught. All of these attitudes and assessments deny us the opportunity to learn from others.

- **Lack of trust.** To learn is to introduce oneself to the unknown, into an action domain in which we accept not knowing. The only way we can get to our destination is to trust our teachers and allow them to guide us. Distrust derails the process. Yet blindly trusting someone to teach us can be folly. What is required is trust with prudence. We reserve the option to withdraw our trust at any point during the process. We continually offer the teacher the opportunity to demonstrate that he or she is worthy of our trust.

As a leader, no matter at what level you are leading (classroom teacher, principal or central office, project team leader, CEO), or in what domain you are leading (education, business, family, community), the ability to learn quickly is critical to effective action in a changing environment. One constant in our world is change: technology itself is evolving at breakneck speed and it is changing how we live our lives almost as quickly; economic conditions are in flux; the political and economic relationships between peoples and countries are shifting continuously. Those who are best able to expand their possibilities for effective action through learning will be the successful leaders of our businesses, our communities, and our governments.

Given that, what gets in the way of your learning as you confront new situations that demand new actions? Do you find it difficult admitting to yourself or others that you don't know something? Do you fail to prioritize for learning and give it enough time in your busy schedule? Do you rigidly hold on to actions that have worked in the past, even though they clearly aren't working now? Do you refuse others permission to teach you? As a leader in your business, your community, in your family, in your personal life, what are your enemies of learning? How can you evade or defeat them in your life?

Reference

Olalla, J. Retrieved from http://www.insightcoaching.com/insights-papers.html

Notes:

LEARNING OPPORTUNITY 5.2

Twelve Principles for Effective Adult Learning

Learning is what occurs within the event, transfer is taking that learning to a new context, and impact is the change in organizations and systems caused by the learning.

—Jane Vella (2008)

Outcome

PLC members will assess how they are learning together based on the twelve principles for effective adult learning theory.

Assumption

Stephen Covey has suggested that in Western culture we are often validated and rewarded for how much we get done. The more we can check off on our to-do lists, the better we feel about ourselves. In a culture of learning, it is not how much we do that is important, but rather how able we are as learners and the extent to which we then choose the right things to do.

Suggested Time

45 minutes

Materials

- "Twelve Principles for Effective Adult Learning" (see p. 160; one copy for each participant)

Learning Event

1. **Set the stage** by asking PLC members to discuss if the principles of learning they apply in their classrooms with their students would be any different from the principles they would apply to adult learning.

2. **Share** with the PLC members that, while there are some similarities in the way adults and young people learn, there are also some differences. To better understand these differences, we can turn to Dr. Jane Vella, a leader in adult learning theory. She researched theorists like Paulo Freire, Malcolm Knowles, Kurt Lewin, and Benjamin Bloom and confirmed that adults learn best through dialogue that takes place in an atmosphere of mutual respect and safety, especially when that dialogue is grounded in the reality of their lives. Through her research, Jane Vella also identified twelve principles for adult learning that help adults become better learners.

3. **Invite** members to access the assessment "Twelve Principles for Effective Adult Learning." Ask them to quietly read the principles and underline key words that stand out as important for each principle. When they have finished reading, ask them to turn to a neighbor and identify one of the twelve principles that feels important to the work of the PLC.

4. **Inquire** if there is anything they are unsure about with regard to the principles or if they have any questions. Once you feel everyone has a basic understanding of the principles, ask them to assess how their PLC has been doing in its learning work up to this point. When they have finished the assessment, ask them to add their total. Ask for a hand count for those who had a score in the excellent category, those in the good category, and so on.

5. **Provide closure** by asking members which principles of the twelve might be worked on to enhance the collaborative learning within the PLC. Once you have agreed on one or two principles that can support the PLC in its learning, name specific steps you can take to draw out more of that principle in the learning work of the PLC.

Future Application

You can use the assessment once a year to gauge the learning growth in the PLC. After a number of years, you will have a longitudinal picture of how members in the PLC are learning together.

Notes:

TWELVE PRINCIPLES FOR EFFECTIVE ADULT LEARNING

In Greek, *dia* means "between," *logos* means "word." Hence, dia + logue = "the word between us." Adult learning is best achieved in dialogue. This is the premise of Jane Vella's research in adult learning theory. Dr. Vella has identified twelve principles to begin, maintain, and nurture the dialogue. The approach to adult learning based on these principles holds that professionals have enough life experience to be in dialogue and to learn together through dialogue. Each of these principles helps guide the PLC in its learning work:

1. Needs Assessment: The First Step in Dialogue

Excellent	Good	Satisfactory	Fair	Poor
5	4	3	2	1

"Who needs what as defined by whom?" In regard to our PLC, how much room do we have to define our own learning needs as we see them in our unique context? How would we rate our PLC for freedom to choose and identify our own learning needs as well as the resources we bring to our work?

2. Safety: Creating a Safe Environment for Learning

Excellent	Good	Satisfactory	Fair	Poor
5	4	3	2	1

The rise and fall of learners' energy is an accurate indicator of their sense of safety. Creating an atmosphere where learners feel safe is an important responsibility of all the PLC members. In a PLC, members need a place where they can be both "creative and critical" in an affirming learning environment. How would you rate your PLC for creating a safe environment for learning?

3. Sound Relationships: The Power of Friendship and Respect

Excellent	Good	Satisfactory	Fair	Poor
5	4	3	2	1

The relationship between PLC members is vital. The more each member can formally and informally create a relationship of mutual respect, the greater the motivation and learning potential for each adult learner. How would you rate the relational factor of respect and mutual regard in your PLC?

4. Sequence and Reinforcement: Knowing Where and How to Begin

Excellent	Good	Satisfactory	Fair	Poor
5	4	3	2	1

Based on the needs assessment, the PLC should design an appropriate sequence of learning moving from simple to complex in a way that reinforces the collective learning of the group. How would you rate your PLC's ability to sequence learning?

5. Praxis: Action with Reflection

Excellent	Good	Satisfactory	Fair	Poor
5	4	3	2	1

Praxis is the Greek word for action with reflection. Praxis is practice in dynamic relation with thought, where the learner engages in the practice of a new skill, attitude, or concept—then immediately reflects on what he or she just did. How well does your PLC do in identifying new strategies for action and then taking time to reflect together on what occurred?

6. Respect for Learners: Learners as Subjects of Their Own Learning

Excellent	Good	Satisfactory	Fair	Poor
5	4	3	2	1

In Swahili, the word "perspective" is translated as "the place where one stands." Dr. Vella holds that a "person's perspective is a holy place to be honored and respected, even if it is different from another's" (p. 139). How do the members of your PLC respect one another's different viewpoints when learning together?

7. Learning with Ideas, Feelings, and Actions

Excellent	Good	Satisfactory	Fair	Poor
5	4	3	2	1

According to the Dr. Vella, every adult learning task should include three things: ideas, feelings, and actions. Is each of these a part of your normal PLC planning and meeting time? If not, which one or two do you include most often? How would you rate your PLC for learning with ideas, feelings and actions?

8. Immediacy: Learning What is Really Useful

Excellent	Good	Satisfactory	Fair	Poor
5	4	3	2	1

In all kinds of adult learning, immediacy is a key motivator! That is, learners must be able to see the immediate usefulness of any learning content for them, in their own unique context. How does your PLC learning time connect to the immediacy of each other's work? How would you rate your PLC for connecting learning to immediacy in supporting adult learning?

9. Clear Roles: Reinforcement of Human Equity

Excellent	Good	Satisfactory	Fair	Poor
5	4	3	2	1

How are roles assigned in your PLC? How do you make sure that roles rotate around the group so someone is not always in the position of being the note taker? How do leadership roles get distributed in the PLC over time? How would you rate your PLC for overall clarity for establishing roles that reinforce human equity?

10. Teamwork: How People Learn Together

Excellent	Good	Satisfactory	Fair	Poor
5	4	3	2	1

Teamwork is an important principle of adult learning! Does it feel like teamwork is a regular part of your PLC learning? Do you learn together as a team around issues that are relevant and timely? How would you rate your PLC for engaging each other in effective teamwork?

11. Engagement: Learning As an Active Process

Excellent	Good	Satisfactory	Fair	Poor
5	4	3	2	1

Without engagement, there is no learning. Adults are engaged by learning that feels significant and relevant to their own work. How would you rate your PLC time for engagement?

12. Accountability: Success Is in the Eyes of the Learner

Excellent	Good	Satisfactory	Fair	Poor
5	4	3	2	1

How does your PLC determine that its learning efforts are successful? What accountability measures do you have in place to measure your success and growth as a PLC? How would you rate your PLC for having accountability measures?

Total	Excellent	Good	Satisfactory	Fair	Poor
	55–60	48–54	36–47	24–35	12–23

Adapted with permission from Jane Vella from her book, *Learning to Listen, Learning to Teach: The Power of Dialogue in Educating Adults* by Jane Vella, published by Jossey-Bass, Inc., Publishers, 1994 (www.globalearning.com)

LEARNING OPPORTUNITY 5.3

The PLC Action Plan

While a plan is essential for understanding where the change journey is moving, it should never be considered to be cast in concrete.

—Hall & Hord (2001)

Outcome

The PLC will develop one action plan for every goal it has.

Assumption

Simply having a goal is not enough in attaining the results for that goal. In order for a goal to be truly realized, a plan has to be put in place that allows for flexibility and sensitivity to the cultural conditions of the workplace.

Suggested Time

1–1.5 hours

Materials

- "The PLC Action Plan" (see p. 165; one copy for each participant)
- Flip chart and markers
- Highlighters

Learning Event

1. **Set the stage** for building an action plan for the PLC in one of the following two ways.

    a. **Use** the Learning Opportunity 3.5, Identifying a PLC Learning Goal. Once the PLC has identified a learning goal, fill out "The PLC Action Plan."

    Or

    b. **Start** by asking PLC members to reference a blank copy of "The PLC Action Plan" as a guide. Ask members to identify Item 1, "School Improvement and/or District Improvement Goals," on flip-chart paper.

        i. **Invite** members to discuss if any of these goals might best be explored and supported by the learning work of the PLC. Highlight in yellow all the district or school goals that the PLC could support.

---

   ii. **Invite** members to list on flip-chart paper their ideas for Item 2 of the PLC Action Plan, the "Classroom or Student Learning Data" they are individually monitoring for improving student learning. You might chart it in the following way:

      Data Source   *Current Results*

   iii. **Direct** members to discuss together and then identify one or two possible PLC learning goals connected to improving student learning in the classroom, school, or district. This conversation may be more helpful if it focuses on *what the PLC members need to learn together or on what topic they want to conduct inquiry* rather than on what members should *do*. The intent is to identify the one or two PLC learning goals that will have the greatest impact on staff learning, which will then be translated into professional behaviors that influence student learning.

2. Write the PLC learning goal in Section 3 of the PLC Action Plan form, "A PLC Learning Goal That Impacts Staff Learning and Will Transfer Into Professional Behaviors That Improve Student Learning."

   An example of PLC learning goals might be the following:

   i. The PLC will *identify* and *learn to use* research-based principles that assist students in retaining and remembering essential learning.

   ii. The PLC will develop instructional practices that are congruent with the research on learning and retention in order to enhance vocabulary development in the school.

3. **Ask** members to work together in completing *one* action plan for each goal they have identified, to help guide their work toward reaching their learning goal. We highly recommend that the PLC have no more than one or two learning goals.

4. **Provide closure** by asking members to reference Learning Opportunity 2.2, A Guide for Making Decisions. Use the decision tree found in that learning opportunity as a guide to consider at what level decisions made around each of the learning goals may have an impact on the school and on other programs.

Future Application

Use "The PLC Action Plan" for building a shared understanding of the PLC's work and how it is having an impact on student learning. The action plan also becomes a communication tool for influencing partners (school board, superintendent, central office) in the learning work of the PLC.

Finally, all PLC agendas should include an update for how the plan is moving forward and how it is making a difference for student learning.

Notes:

③ A PLC Learning Goal That Impacts Staff Learning and Will Transfer Into Professional Behaviors That Improve Student Learning	② Classroom or Student Learning Data		① School Improvement and/or District Improvement Goals
	Data Source	*Current Results*	
④ List the data you will monitor and collect that reveals how your professional learning is having an impact on student learning:	Resources Needed:		Timelines:

Stakeholders	Who is Responsible	What we are doing now . . . (current)	What we want to do . . . (desired)	Barriers	Boosters
PLC Member Action Steps: 1. 2.					
Principal Action Steps: 1. 2.					
Central Office Action Steps: 1. 2.					

166

LEARNING OPPORTUNITY 5.4

Listening Together in the PLC

Burley-Allen (1995) notes that in communicating we spend 9 percent of our time writing, 16 percent of our time reading, 35 percent of our time speaking, and 40 percent of our time listening. So, we ask, where do we teach listening in schools? How do we teach listening skills to the adults? How do we practice active listening in our professional learning communities?

—Hord & Sommers (2008)

Outcome

PLC members will describe seven different types of listening filters and how to apply them with intentionality in their communicating together.

Assumption

If we can't move a conversation toward what we want, a lot of wasted time and energy is spent in unproductive dialogue and discussion. Being able to move a conversation is dependent on how we are listening.

Suggested Time

30 minutes

Materials

- Scissors (one pair for each participant)
- "The Listening Voice" (see p. 169; one copy for each participant)
- "Listening Filters" (copied on white card stock) (see p. 171; one copy for each participant)

Learning Event

1. **Set the stage** by sharing the following quote with PLC members, "Perhaps one of the most precious and powerful gifts we can give another person is to really listen to them, to listen . . . with our whole being. This sounds simple, but if we are honest with ourselves, we do not often listen to each other so completely." (Kay Lindahl, *The Sacred Art of Listening*, p. 11)

   Ask PLC members to discuss this question: "What might make listening such a difficult thing to do, especially in the workplace?"

Inform PLC members that today's learning opportunity will focus on seven different ways we can listen, when working and learning together in the PLC. Each form of listening has its purpose; when chosen wisely, each form can make all the difference in how PLC members communicate with each other.

2. **Ask** PLC members to find a learning partner to work with whom to read "The Listening Voice." Instruct the partners to read one paragraph at a time. At the end of reading each paragraph, one partner does a modified version of a *think aloud*. The partner shares out loud what he or she was thinking during and after the reading of the paragraph. There are four paragraphs so partners will share their thinking out loud twice.

3. **Begin the dialogue** by asking participants (when everyone has finished reading) what important learning they want to remember regarding listening and communicating with each other. You might post these ideas on flip-chart paper.

4. **Distribute** "Listening Filters," copied on card stock. Ask each member to cut out the seven filters and to create a simple table tent for each filter. After the table tents are created, members should carefully read the seven listening filters.

5. **Provide closure** by asking PLC members in what situations it might make sense to apply a specific filter. You might have members write those situations on the backside of the table tent as a reminder.

Finally, have members begin to notice their preferred listening filter as you work through other agenda items you had planned to cover in the meeting. At the end of the meeting, have members report their preferred listening filter. If there is not enough time, you can always bring this back to a future PLC meeting.

Future Application

You might ask PLC members to declare the type(s) of listening that would be most helpful in accomplishing the PLC meeting agenda prior to the meeting. In some cases, you might even use a letter code to identify the different kinds of listening and put the listening code next to items on the meeting agenda that could help signal the communication that could be the most productive.

You might also reference the listening filters when you notice tension or conflict that is not helpful to the group. When this happens, ask members to pull out their listening filters and to decide which filter might be the most helpful in moving the conversation forward.

This simple pause and reflection can often help the PLC to get back on track and improve communication.

Notes:

THE LISTENING VOICE

James L. Roussin

How easily you can belong to everything simply by listening.

—David Whyte

The benefit of collaborative communication, especially in the workplace, is gathering as many perspectives as possible, in order to fashion a more accurate representation of the world. So, in conversation it is always helpful to remember that you only hold a piece of the collective picture you are experiencing in that moment. Your perceptions contain a degree of distortion and generalization based upon the personal filter you are using to make sense of your world. Each perceptual filter organizes meaning based on past experiences and present-moment conditions. While you have many perceptual filters, one that has a significant influence on your communication is your listening filter. A listening filter organizes meaning and gives shape to the conversation by sorting what is being heard. That sorting process is influenced by seven different styles of listening. When you can notice the filter that is framing the meaning in the conversation, you can choose to listen differently in order to enhance communication.

For example, you attend a meeting that has on the agenda a controversial topic that stirs a lot of emotion for you. As you enter the room, you may notice yourself preparing a mental story for how you see the situation and whom you may need to confront to fortify your position. What you may not realize is that you are forming a listening filter based on a perception that is grounded in judgment. That filter shapes the way you hear, how you will make sense of the conversation and how you will choose to respond. Once you are conscious of your listening filters, e.g., listening from a place of judgment, you can begin to intentionally choose a different filter in your listening. So, consider a similar situation where you attend a controversial meeting, but this time you intentionally choose a different listening filter before entering the room. You might choose an empathic filter for example. During the meeting you now hear information differently. You notice the emotional nuances in the conversation. You hear how the topic impacts others in ways different from yourself. And, when you choose to speak, you select a voice that radiates from an empathic position.

Listening filters are especially important when communication becomes reactive and emotionally charged. Perhaps you have been at a meeting when someone stands up with a surly tone and plants his or her opinion toward another with sarcasm. This type of communication can elicit either defensiveness or withdrawal from others. Many times an emotionally loaded response is triggered by how you are listening. If you want to experience a more productive and collaborative workplace, start to notice how you are listening, especially when emotion rises up in the conversation; and then see if you can switch to a listening filter that will enhance the communication.

Finally, the psychologist, R. D. Laing eloquently stated that, *"The range of what we think and do is limited by what we fail to notice. And because we fail to notice that we fail to notice, there is little we can do to change; until we notice how failing to notice shapes our thoughts and deeds."* You can build more awareness into the ways you are responding by tracking your listening filter. So in your next interaction, invite yourself to become aware of the kind of listening you have activated in the conversation. The table on pages xx–xx identifies seven listening filters that you can track. This is not something you have to do every time you are in conversation, but when you notice that the communication between yourself and others is not as productive as you would like it to be, check your listening filter. By noticing your listening, you can intentionally change the ways you communicate with others. Finally, take a look at the list of listening filters on pp. 171–172 and ask yourself which filter shows up the most in your life. If you can manage your listening filter, you can choose how to best engage others in powerful communication that builds trust, supports collaboration, and enhances negotiated meaning for future action and learning.

References

Adams, M. G. (2004). *Change your questions, change your life.* New York: Ballantine.

Adler, R., & Towne, N. (2002). *Looking out/looking in* (10th ed.). New York: Harcourt Brace.

Dweck, C. S. (2006). *Mindset: The new psychology of success.* Somerville, MA: Wisdom.

Orem, S., Binkert, J., & Clancy, A. (2007). *Appreciative coaching.* San Francisco: Jossey-Bass.

Notes

Listening Filters (Table Tent Cards)

LISTENING FILTER	DEFINITION	VERBAL RESPONSE	FOCUS QUESTION
Appreciative	It is from the **appreciative** listening filter that we embrace the *reflected best self* of the speaker. In this type of listening we acknowledge in others their best positive selves. The listener reflects extraordinary moments and dispositions in another's life. This type of listening is a social resource for drawing out the best in each other in a strength-based context.	Exposing the best in others	What do I value about the speaker?
Learning	Carol Dweck, a professor at Stanford, suggests that those who hold a *growth mindset* think positively and are not afraid to make mistakes. They are also able to learn faster and overcome obstacles more easily. When we listen from a **learning** filter we establish a positive intention for whatever we are hearing, and we take a researcher's stance toward life and learning. It is from this filter that we construct meaning through reflection and learn from our experiences.	Progressive versus regressive	What can I learn from the speaker?
Empathic	*Empathy* is derived from the German word Einfühlung, which means "feeling into." This type of listening communicates care and acceptance. It also acknowledges the other person's self worth through the act of listening and the expression of empathy. So at the heart of **empathic** listening is understanding.	Clarifying what the other person has said and responding with empathy	How can I empathize with the speaker?

LISTENING FILTER	DEFINITION	VERBAL RESPONSE	FOCUS QUESTION
Auto-biographical	**Autobiographical** listening is relational listening. It is the means by which we connect to another person by finding something familiar in his or her life. It is probably the most common filter we use for listening. It is through this filter that we can begin to expose who we are and reveal some of our own vulnerability, tentativeness, and hope in a reciprocal relationship. This filter is often the first path to building trust.	My personal story or my experiences, or both	How are the speaker and I the same/different?
Analyzing	When we listen from the **analyzing** filter, we tend to offer an interpretation of what we've heard. You might state to the speaker, "He is doing it because . . ." or "I think what is going on for you is . . ." The challenge with interpretive listening is that we often have limited information from which to interpret another's situation.	Interpretation of the speaker's message or situation	What is the speaker saying/meaning?
Advising	It is common from this listening position to want to help the person out of where he or she is stuck by offering a solution or crafting questions toward what we see as a possible solution. A consequence of the **advising** filter is that the person does not identify her or his own internal resourcefulness in finding a solution that is self-directed.	Identifying and offering a solution	How can I be most helpful to the speaker?
Judging	When we listen from the **judging** filter, we tend to evaluate what is said as being either "right" or "wrong" or "good" or "bad." A judgment is usually easier to receive when the speaker has requested it. Also, a judgment may be better received in the form of constructive criticism about performance or behavior rather than about the person.	Expressing a positive or negative assessment or judgment	How can I improve the speaker's message?

LEARNING OPPORTUNITY 5.5

Using the Stages of Concern to Connect Professional Learning to the Classroom

All changes, even the most longed for, have their melancholy; for what we leave behind is part of ourselves; we must die to one life before we can enter another one.

—Anatole France

Outcome

Participants will demonstrate the use of Stages of Concern (SoC) to support PLC members in applying what they have learned in the PLC to their classrooms.

Assumption

We believe the purpose of the PLC is to connect learning in the PLC to the classroom, where it can improve students' learning and inform our community learning.

Suggested Time

Two sessions of 1 hour each, with the first hour for SoC overview and data collection. Before the second session, SoC data will be compiled and given to staff with adequate time for each staff person's individual analysis. The second session includes 1 hour for debriefing and reflection, as described in the Future Applications section.

Materials

- "Stages of Concern (SoC) Learning Opportunity Handout" (see p. 176; one copy for each participant)
- "Stages of Concern Chart with Related Expressions of Concern" (see p. 178; one copy for each participant)
- "Corresponding School Graph for SoC" (see p. 178; one copy for each participant)
- A poster-size copy of "Corresponding School Graph for SoC" for recording of teachers' concerns in Step 3
- pp. 117–121 of *Leading Professional Learning Communities: Voices From Research and Practice* (Hord & Sommers, 2008)

Learning Event

1. **Set the stage** by asking participants to write one complete sentence expressing their concerns about the implementation of their new curriculum or program. Collect the

responses on chart paper. These sentences provide insight into the current state of individuals in the implementation process.

2. **Distribute** and invite participants to read the SoC Learning Opportunity Handout. Provide participants with all Stages of Concern (SoC) materials, and guide them in their reading of it, providing opportunities for them to ask questions for clarification. Review the SoC information with the group. Explain that our school will be collecting school-wide data from math teachers using the Stages of Concern, and subsequently on the Levels of Use (LoU). Resulting data from the two tools will be used as indicators to plan interventions, appraise progress, and determine professional learning. Teachers will have different concerns, progress through changes in different ways, and thus will be in different stages.

3. **Use** the sentences each teacher wrote during Step 1, to practice rating or scoring their concerns. They will determine their Stages of Concern for their current level of implementation of the new curriculum or program by using the SoC Chart. They then mark an X on the enlarged school graph corresponding to their concerns (refer to the SoC chart in the materials). An option can be to identify each grade-level or math course concerns with a different color to see not only the individual staff members' respective Stages of Concern, but also see the data by grade level or math course.

4. **Facilitate** reflective conversations about the data represented on the graph through selecting appropriate questions for discussion:
   - What do the data tell us?
   - Where are our concerns in mathematics?
   - From reviewing the data on the school line plot or bar graph, how can we describe the school?
   - How can these data influence our teaching practice?
   - Based on this data reflection process, what would be useful next steps?
   - What support do you need as a teacher?
   - What could the *collaboration level* of the SoC look like in your teaching practice?
   - What did you learn in using the Stages of Concern?

5. **Provide closure** by asking PLC members to reflect in writing on the following questions:
   - What is my biggest concern about the math implementation process?
   - What is my "next step" in the math implementation process?
   - What support do I need to get there?

Future Applications

Compile the data results from Step 5 (above) and provide a copy of the results back to the teachers and administrators before the second SoC session. Ask participants to review the SoC handouts and invite them to further analyze the data and specify any questions. Teachers are encouraged to delineate the next steps for professional learning and bring their suggestions to the next SoC session. The data, questions, feedback from participants, and reflective dialogue will help deepen the teachers' understanding of the SoC tool and its applications to their teaching practices.

In this second 1-hour session, PLC members bring the data that they were given and their analyses of it. Solicit their questions and conduct discussion across the group to respond to the questions. Take good care here to clarify misunderstandings and to support the group in their learning about Stages of Concern and how they can use it in their implementation of the new math curriculum.

In their small groups, invite them to share their analyses, come to a group conclusion about their analysis and report to the large group. Correct misinterpretations and clarify their misunderstandings regarding their synthesis.

Invite participants to share their suggestions for next steps, asking them to consider them in light of their conclusions about the data. Bring closure to this discussion by making a decision about what the next steps actually will be for the community.

Notes:

This Learning Opportunity is based on the work of Gene Hall, Shirley Hord, and others and was developed by Cathy J. Kinzer, assistant professor at New Mexico State University (NMSU), in collaboration with Laura Taft, professional development teacher for Las Cruces (NM) Public School, and Sheila Hills, project coordinator with Mathematically Connected Communities at NMSU.

STAGES OF CONCERN (SoC) LEARNING OPPORTUNITY HANDOUT

There is and will always be a critical place for consideration of the individual in the change process.

—Susan Loucks-Horsley and Suzanne Stiegelbauer

Background

A school district has decided to implement a problem-solving-based mathematics curriculum. The district takes the stance that a constructivist orientation to teaching and learning would best support the goal of their students becoming critical thinkers and problem solvers, and to be able to communicate their mathematical ideas effectively. There are eight schools in this district: one high school, one middle school, and six elementary schools. Six of the schools have launched the use of the new math curriculum, while two have not, these being Alan Middle School and Beatrice Elementary School.

> It is a new mathematics program for the school and therefore requires changes in both teaching and leadership practices. The Concerns-Based Adoption Model (CBAM), (Hall & Hord, 2006) is a model that provides tools that predict the development of individuals in a change effort. CBAM tools can be used to assess change and determine interventions for addressing both the emotional side of change as well as behavioral side. (Hord & Sommers, 2008, pp. 118–121)

In supporting professional learning, it is essential to consider where teachers, both individually and as a group, are in a change effort and to determine the assistance required to meet their professional learning needs. The goal of the adult learning is to promote student learning.

The kinds of concerns, behaviors, and questions that individual teachers or administrators express can provide important data for understanding their needs in the change process. Specifically, CBAM (Concerns-Based Adoption Model) tools—LoU and SoC—are useful for assessing where individual teachers are in the implementation of the new math program, providing indicators of changes. The research (Hall & Hord, 2006) delineates that the types of questions and concerns usually move from a focus on one's self to the task or activity, and ultimately to focus on the impact of the innovation to promote student learning. The CBAM tools afford ways to gather data and assess where teachers are in the change process, so that leaders, facilitators, and teachers can make informed choices for mentoring and providing professional learning to the individual implementers.

Learning Opportunities 5.5 and 5.6 provide processes that can be used with a whole-school PLC with follow-up in team PLCs; it also can be modified based on need. After teachers become familiar with the CBAM tools, they determine their LoU or SoC. Each individual is represented in the aggregate data snapshot of the LoU or SoC. The graph represents a current snapshot of where the school staff is in relation to the SoC or LoU.

The next step is to analyze the data and determine what actions are needed to provide relevant support to meet teachers' needs. It is important to continually assess and monitor the state of individuals and determine the appropriate interventions to support them in their learning journey. Teachers can prepare to support each other as they transfer their PLC learning to their classrooms. The ultimate shared goal is student learning.

Context

Alan Middle School is late in beginning the implementation of the district-required mathematics curriculum. The school has been dealing with bigger issues regarding the new school boundaries that have redistributed teachers and students. There is a need for understanding the current state of the new curriculum's implementation process through the teachers' perspectives. This is needed to determine support for the math teachers. The SoC will be used with the teachers as they *begin* to transfer or implement the new curriculum in their classrooms. The SoC will be used several other times throughout the implementation process to provide data about the teachers' concerns regarding the curriculum.

The SoC is a useful tool for the PLC to help understand the teachers' concerns regarding the implementation process. Each individual has a set of beliefs, feelings, and apprehensions about change—these are their concerns. These concerns need to be brought to the fore in the change process in order to acknowledge and respond appropriately to the teachers' and administrators' needs. The SoC model has seven developmental stages (Awareness to Refocusing), described by their related expressions of concern. People move through these stages as they implement changes.

Notes:

STAGES OF CONCERN CHART WITH RELATED EXPRESSIONS OF CONCERN

Stages of Concern	Typical Expressions of Concern
6. Refocusing	I have some ideas about something that would work even better.
5. Collaboration	How can I relate what I am doing to what others are doing?
4. Consequence	How is my use affecting learners? How can I refine it to have more impact?
3. Management	I seem to be spending all my time getting materials ready.
2. Personal	How will using it affect me?
1. Informational	I would like to know more about it.
0. Awareness	I am not concerned about it.

Adapted with permission of SEDL. Hord, S. M., Rutherford, W. L., Huling-Austin, L., & Hall, G. E. (2004). *Taking charge of change* (Rev. ed). Austin, TX: Southwest Educational Development Laboratory.

CORRESPONDING SCHOOL GRAPH FOR SoC

Example Line Plot for *SoC* with each teacher represented by a discrete X on the graph

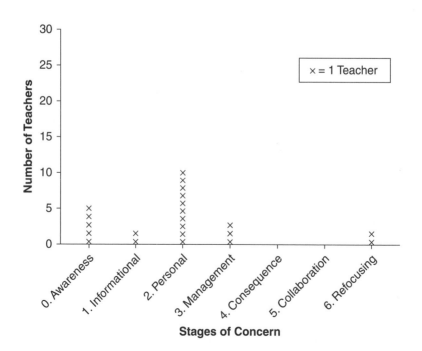

LEARNING OPPORTUNITY 5.6

Using the Levels of Use (LoU) to Connect Professional Learning to the Classroom

It doesn't work to leap a twenty-foot chasm in two ten-foot jumps.

—American proverb

Outcome

The PLC members will identify teachers' LoU as they implement new practices, including new curriculum and instructional strategies; provide appropriate support for the use of the new practices; and, thus, provide more effective teaching and learning.

Assumption

Leaders, who observe implementers' behaviors when they are implementing an initiative, have the basis to respond appropriately to their learning needs. The LoU is a resource that can make the change process visible and help school leaders provide relevant professional learning.

Suggested Time

One hour will be needed for this initial LoU activity. Additionally, one hour will be needed at a subsequent PLC meeting to review the schoolwide data generated from this learning opportunity, discuss and analyze the data, and make suggestions for improved implementation.

Materials

- "Levels of Use (LoU) Definitions With Decision Points" (see p. 182; one copy for each participant)
- A poster-size copy of "School Graph for LoU" (see p. 184; one copy for each participant)
- pp. 121–122 of *Leading Professional Learning Communities: Voices From Research and Practice* (Hord & Sommers, 2008)

Learning Event

The PLC session will use the first 10 minutes to review the artifacts summarizing their learning from the previous SoC learning opportunities.

1. **Set the stage** by asking participants to choose a partner with whom to work. Each person in the partnership will take 3 minutes to describe to their colleague: (a) if they are using the newly adopted curriculum, or whatever the new practice, and (b) how they use it in their teaching.

Background: Beatrice Elementary School is just beginning the implementation process of a district-required curriculum. All teachers are required to use the problem-solving-based curriculum. The curricular materials were not all received at the onset of the school year and most teachers did not have training on how to use these resources. Additionally, the instructional coach has only recently taken this position at Beatrice Elementary School. Teachers have expressed a need about their curriculum content expertise and most teachers have never used a problem-solving-based curriculum in their classrooms. The coach wants to determine where teachers are in the implementation process and provide the types of professional learning that will meet their needs. The SoC and LoU will be used as tools to periodically assess the teachers' concerns and use of the new curriculum to assess its implementation.

2. **Share** and solicit PLC member contributions to a discussion about the importance in knowing where each person is in the curriculum implementation process, in order to plan and provide the needed support. The LoU is a tool to identify the uses of curricular materials, assess progress of implementation, and afford the appropriate support for teachers to use the materials effectively.

3. **Using** the LoU definitions, invite participants to share their mental images of each of the LoU. They collaboratively discuss and codevelop shared visual images of what LoU 1 would look like, and continue for each LoU. The shared mental images for each of the LoU are represented on a poster; the visualization represents what it would look like for each of the LoU. Then, each person determines their individual level on the LoU chart and marks the respective level on the enlarged school graph.

4. **Facilitate** reflective PLC conversations about the data represented on the LoU graph through questions such as:

   o What do the data tell us?
   o What support do you need to implement the curriculum effectively?
   o Based on the overall reported levels, what types of professional development or learning are needed?
   o Are there any notable relationships between your SoC and LoU data?
   o What would a classroom look like if students had opportunities to become effective problem solvers in their subjects?
   o What would it take as a staff to be focused on professional collaboration that promotes student learning?
   o What did you learn through exploring the LoU?

5. **Provide closure** by requesting that each PLC participant uses a 3–2–1 reflection to respond in writing to these questions.

   o What are **three** things you learned from this LoU process?
   o Describe **two** challenges or barriers that you face in implementing the curriculum.
   o What is **one** question you have about our new program?

Future Application

Compile the schoolwide data that represent the teachers' LoU, and provide a copy of the results to all staff. These LoU data can be organized in a table, chart, or in whatever arrangement would be useful to the particular school. Ask staff to study, analyze, and state conclusions regarding the data.

The next PLC meeting affords the opportunity for dialogue and focused conversations regarding the LoU. Participants will be asked to examine the data and their written reflections and to provide suggestions for the learning journey. These ideas will be used to develop professional learning opportunities for guiding the change efforts.

The information from SoC and LoU data, from teachers' questions, from classroom observations (by the coach, other teachers, principal), and staff dialogue will be analyzed over time to provide appropriate professional learning, teacher support, and encouragement. The SoC and LoU tools can empower educators as they become more aware of the indicators and progression of change encountered in the implementation process.

Notes:

This Learning Opportunity was codeveloped by Cathy Kinzer, assistant professor at New Mexico State University (NMSU), in collaboration with Laura Taft, a professional development teacher for Las Cruces, New Mexico, Public Schools, and Sheila Hills, a project coordinator with Mathematically Connected Communities at NMSU.

LEVELS OF USE (LoU) DEFINITIONS WITH DECISION POINTS

Describes or operationally defines the behaviors of the users of the innovation through various stages

Level 0—Non-Use

State in which the individual has little or no involvement with it and is doing nothing toward becoming involved.

Decision Point A—Takes action to learn more detailed information about the innovation.

Level I—Orientation

State in which the individual has acquired or is acquiring the information about the innovation or has explored its value orientation and what it will require.

Decision Point B—Makes a decision to use the innovation by establishing a time to begin.

Level II—Preparation

State in which the user is preparing for the first use of the innovation.

Decision Point C—Begins first use of the innovation.

Level III—Mechanical Use

State in which the user focuses most effort of the short-term, day-to-day use of the innovation with little time for reflection. Changes in use are made more to meet user needs than needs of students and others. The user is primarily engaged in an attempt to master tasks required to do the innovation. These attempts often result in disjointed and superficial use.

Decision Point D-1—A routine pattern of use is established.

Level IVA—Routine

Use of the innovation is stabilized. Few if any changes are being made in ongoing use. Little preparation or thought is given to improve the innovation use or its consequences.

Decision Point D-2—Changes use of the innovation based on formal and informal evaluation in order to increase client outcomes.

Level IVB—Refinement

State in which the user varies the use of the innovation to increase impact on clients (students or others) within their immediate sphere of influence. Variations in use are based on knowledge of both short- and long-term consequences for clients.

Decision Point E—Initiates changes in use of the innovation based on input from and in coordination with colleagues for benefit of clients.

Level V— Integration

State in which the user is combining own efforts to use the innovation with related activities of colleagues to achieve a collective impact on clients within their common sphere of influence.

Decision Point F—Begins exploring alternatives of the innovation presently in use.

Level VI—Renewal

State in which the user reevaluates the quality of the use of the innovation, seeks modifications of the innovation to achieve increased impact on clients, examines new developments in the field, and explores new goals for self or the organization.

Levels of Use	Behavioral Indicators of Level
VI. Renewal	The user is seeking more effective alternatives to the established use of the innovation.
V. Integration	The user is making deliberate efforts to coordinate with others in using the innovation.
IVB. Refinement	The user is making changes to increase outcomes.
IVA. Routine	The user is making few or no changes and has an established pattern of use.
III. Mechanical	The user is making changes to better organize use of the innovation.
II. Preparation	The user has definite plans to begin using the innovation.
I. Orientation	The user is taking the initiative to learn more about the innnovation.
0. Non-Use	The user has no interest and is taking no action.

Adapted with permission of SEDL. Hord, S. M., Rutherford, W. L., Huling-Austin, L. & Hall, G. E. (2004). *Taking charge of change* (Rev. ed.). Austin, TX: Southwest Educational Development Laboratory.

SCHOOL GRAPH FOR LoU

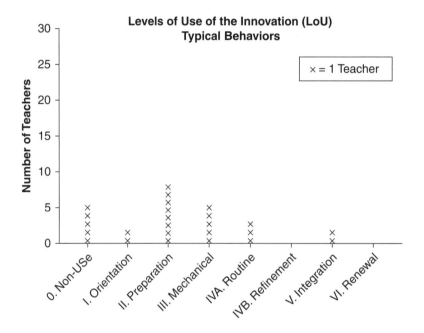

LEARNING OPPORTUNITY 5.7

PLC Growth Development Profile

By using the term professional learning community we signify our interest not only in discrete acts of teacher sharing, but in the establishment of a schoolwide culture that makes collaboration expected, inclusive, genuine, ongoing, and focused on critically examining practice to improve student outcomes . . . The hypothesis is that what teachers do together outside of the classroom can be as important as what they do inside in affecting school restructuring, teachers' professional development, and student learning.

—K. Seashore, A. Anderson, E. Riedel, *Implementing Arts for Academic Achievement* (2003)

Outcome

The PLC will assess its developmental growth around nine factors in order to identify ways in which the PLC matures.

Assumption

There are research-based factors that promote the growth and sustainability of a successful PLC, especially with regard to influencing student learning. A PLC doesn't evolve out of happenstance. It evolves out of intentionality through self-monitoring and assessment.

Suggested Time

30 minutes

Materials

- "PLC Growth Development Profile" (see p. 187; one copy for each participant)
- Flip-chart paper and markers

Learning Event

1. **Set the stage** by asking PLC members to reflect on the question, "how do members determine if growth is occurring in the PLC?" Ask them to identify one or more factors that might be monitored to determine whether the PLC is growing or stagnant.

2. **Hand out** "PLC Growth Development Profile" to each member. Ask them to look at nine of twelve factors identified by Bolam et al. for sustainable PLCs. Invite them to discuss why these nine factors might be important to the growth and sustainability of a PLC.

How effective is our PLC? ➜	Shared values and vision	Collective responsibility for student learning	Collaboration focused on learning	Professional learning, individual and collective	Reflective professional inquiry	Openness, networks, and partnerships	Mutual trust, respect, and support	Optimization of resources and structures to promote the work of the PLC	Evaluating the effectiveness of the PLC

Source: Bolam et al. (2005, p. 154)

3. **Next**, ask members to assess each of the factors in their PLC by rating them at one of four levels:

   o **Seeding and Germinating:** This factor is not present or is just in the beginning stage.

   o **Sprouting:** This factor is just starting to take hold and is present in the PLC.

   o **Flowering & Pollination:** This factor is very present and is currently blossoming in the PLC. It might even be a core value.

   o **Death or Regeneration:** This factor has outlived its time and/or is in need of renewal.

4. **Post** all of the growth development profiles on a wall where PLC members can take a gallery walk and see how each member assessed the current growth level of the PLC.

5. **Provide closure** by asking members what needs to happen next to nurture more growth in the PLC and create sustainability. You might start this by asking members to quietly journal on their assessment forms in the space labeled "suggestions for maturing the PLC." Chart the information on flip-chart paper. After all of the ideas are shared, have members vote on two or three of the suggestions that should be the focus for future PLC meetings.

Future Application

You might assign one of the nine growth factors to each PLC member. That member then becomes a process observer for the group and offers feedback at the end of the meeting. We would suggest that you only focus on one or two growth factors per meeting as a form of feedback.

Also, each person could develop a list of critical attributes for his/her factor that could be seen by group members when the PLC is operating at its best.

Notes:

PLC Growth Development Profile

Create a line graph to chart where you perceive your PLC is in terms of development in the following growth areas.

How effective is our PLC?	Shared values and vision	Collective responsibility for student learning	Collaboration focused on learning	Professional learning. individual and collective	Reflective professional inquiry	Openness, networks, and partnerships	Mutual trust, respect, and support	Optimization of resources and structures to promote the work of the PLC	Evaluating the effectiveness of the PLC
Seeding and Germinating	●	●	●	●	●	●	●	●	●
Sprouting [Roots and Stems]	●	●	●	●	●	●	●	●	●
Flowering & Pollination	●	●	●	●	●	●	●	●	●
Death or Regeneration	●	●	●	●	●	●	●	●	●

Component **6**

Sharing Personal Practice

OVERVIEW AND CURRENT THINKING

Sharing one's classroom practice is more than just reporting to colleagues about an activity or procedure for helping Johnny read more successfully—that might be termed sharing expertise, or sharing repertoire. The major focus of this component is a bit more formal. For example, a host teacher invites a visiting teacher to come to his or her classroom at an appointed time to observe an identified action or behavior. The visiting teacher observes, scripts notes, and discusses the observations with the host teacher after the visit. This activity is in the spirit of peers supporting peers. Both the host and the visiting teacher grow from the experience of observing, and giving and receiving feedback. This process contributes to individuals' and consequently to the organization's improvement.

In the process, teachers reflect on their practice with the help of their colleagues and fine-tune their instructional practices. To be successful, a workplace culture that promotes respect and understanding is *de rigueur.* It is a culture where teachers celebrate each other's successes and offer each other empathy and support when difficulties evolve. This is a culture where teachers encourage discussion, debate, and disagreement. The staff finds support for each other's triumphs and troubles.

Note: These introductory passages for Components 1–6 have been enhanced by the work of Dr. Sue Greer, Superintendent of Schools, of the District School Board of Niagara, Ontario, Canada.

LEARNING OPPORTUNITY 6.1

"Foursight" for Learning: Four Focus Areas to Consider in Monitoring for Student Learning

An unrelenting attention to student learning success is the core characteristic of the learning community of professionals.

—Louis & Kruse (1995)

Outcome

PLC members will identify and explore four key areas of student learning to assist them in determining where to focus their own learning work.

Assumption

Student learning is much more than how students are performing on state tests or making their way through classroom curriculum. We might think of student learning as a compass that has four clear directions for learning development: Cognition, Psychomotor, Emotions, and Socialization.

Suggested Time

45–60 minutes

Materials

- Flip chart and markers
- "Foursight for Learning" (see p. 192; one copy for each participant)

Learning Event

Note: This learning opportunity might be useful just before setting a PLC learning goal.

1. Set the stage by referring to the graphic and text from Hord & Sommer's book, *Leading Professional Communities*. You might ask PLC members if the graphic makes sense to them and what questions they might be asking themselves as they think about their own work in the PLC?

   In order to reach the desired student learning outcomes, we "backward map." We identify the desired learning outcomes for students (1) and then consider staff learning (2), which

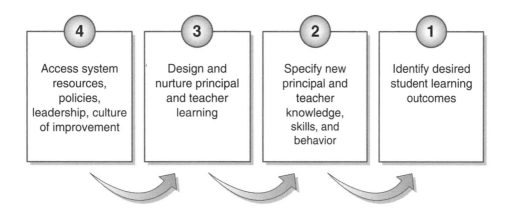

precedes student learning (1). In the PLC, staff give attention to professional learning and development (3) that will support what they need to learn in order to prepare themselves to work more effectively for students. Factors in the system (4) contribute to this theory of change by providing resources, leadership, policies, a culture of continuous improvement, and others (Hord & Sommers, 2008).

2. **Distribute** "Foursight for Learning." Ask each member to identify in each quadrant what he or she thinks would be reliable data that one could reference to determine how students were performing in their learning. You can have them do this with partners or quietly by themselves. After they have had some time to think about this, use the flip-chart paper to brainstorm about where to find evidence of student learning in these four directions.

If you have enough PLC members, you might ask for volunteers who would scan, monitor, analyze, and report data to the PLC throughout the year. It is our contention that by paying attention to all four areas of learning you can better leverage success in one particular area that is in need of improvement.

3. **Provide closure** by engaging a conversation around which of the four focus areas might be the most important for leveraging improvements in the overall performance of students. These four areas of learning do not stand alone. They are interwoven into a developmental pattern that supports and nurtures the growth and learning of all students.

Future Application

You might enlarge the "Foursight for Learning" graphic and have it posted in the PLC room. This can be a reminder when discussing student learning data that learning means more than the cognitive ability of students. You could also do an artifact hunt (posters, student work, etc.) in the school to identify examples of where the school celebrates and engages students in these four areas of learning.

Notes:

FOURSIGHT FOR LEARNING

"Emotions enable a child to master symbols. . . The symbolic use of language, in turn, creates the foundation for more advanced social and intellectual capacities, including higher and higher levels of reflective thinking."
The First Idea by Stanley Greenspan and Stuart Shanker (2004)

Emotions and Learning

Psychomotor learning is demonstrated by physical skills; coordination, dexterity, manipulation, grace, strength, speed; actions which demonstrate the fine motor skills such as use of precision instruments or tools, or actions which evidence gross motor skills such as the use of the body in dance or athletic performance. *from "The Distance Learning, Technology Resource Guide," by Carla Lane*

Psychomotor Skills and Learning

Monitoring Student Achievement

Cognition and Learning

The cognitive domain involves knowledge and the development of intellectual skills. This includes the recall or recognition of specific facts, procedural patterns, and concepts that serve in the development on intellectual abilities and skills. There are six major categories and can be thought of as degrees of difficulties. Bloom B. S. (1956)

Socialization and Learning

Vygotsky (1978) states: "Every function in the child's cultural development appears twice: first, on the social level, and later, on the individual level; first, between people (interpsychological) and then inside the child (intrapsychological). This applies equally to voluntary attention, to logical memory, and to the formation of concepts. All the higher functions originate as actual relationships between individuals." (p57).

LEARNING OPPORTUNITY 6.2

Four Conversations

Making mental connections is our most crucial learning tool: the essence of human intelligence; to forge links; to go beyond the given; to see patterns, relationships, context.

—Marilyn Ferguson

Outcome

Learners will identify four conversation modes, be aware of the kind of conversation that is happening, and be able to change the conversation to enhance our learning.

Assumption

We sometimes get stuck in conversations that take time and end up being less productive. By recognizing the kind of conversation that is taking place and knowing the kind of conversation that may lead to greater learning, we can proactively increase learning and motivation.

Suggested Time

1–1.5 hours

Materials

- "Four Conversations" (see p. 194; one copy for each participant)

Learning Event

1. **Set the stage** by inviting participants to provide examples of the four kinds of conversations identified on the handout "Four Conversations."

2. **Discuss** the following questions: What percentage of time do we spend in each category while in the PLC? Which category results in the most learning in our PLC? What are some ways we can increase the time spent in the most productive category when we meet? How might the agenda reflect the categories?

3. **Provide closure** by identifying a person to track the time the PLC group spends in each category during the remainder of the meeting. Where did the most learning occur?

Future Application

What other places would be useful to use this application? How might we use this to increase meaning and decrease time in unproductive conversations in other venues?

FOUR CONVERSATIONS

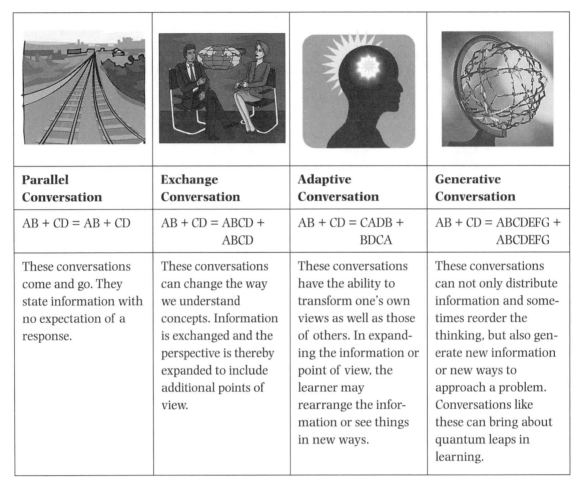

Parallel Conversation	Exchange Conversation	Adaptive Conversation	Generative Conversation
AB + CD = AB + CD	AB + CD = ABCD + ABCD	AB + CD = CADB + BDCA	AB + CD = ABCDEFG + ABCDEFG
These conversations come and go. They state information with no expectation of a response.	These conversations can change the way we understand concepts. Information is exchanged and the perspective is thereby expanded to include additional points of view.	These conversations have the ability to transform one's own views as well as those of others. In expanding the information or point of view, the learner may rearrange the information or see things in new ways.	These conversations can not only distribute information and sometimes reorder the thinking, but also generate new information or new ways to approach a problem. Conversations like these can bring about quantum leaps in learning.

Notes:

LEARNING OPPORTUNITY 6.3

Coaching: Transferring Adult Learning to the Classroom or What's Learned Here Leaves Here

Even if you're on the right track, you'll get run over if you just sit there.

—Will Rogers

Outcome

Learners will identify 10 roles of coaching, state their definitions, and describe an application of each role in the school.

Assumption

Just as champion golfers and other athletic stars retain a coach, so should such persons be available to respond to administrators' and teachers' individual and idiosyncratic concerns, questions, and needs as they implement new practice(s) in their efforts to continually increase their effectiveness.

Suggested Time

2 hours

Materials

- Flip chart and markers
- "The Ten Roles of Coaches" (see p. 197; one copy for each participant)
- "Adult Learning and Implementing New Practice in Classrooms" (see p. 200; one copy for each participant)

Learning Event

1. **Set the stage** by soliciting from participants what they know or have experienced about teacher support coaches, their roles, and the effect that any of the coaches has had on classroom practice. Record responses on a flip chart; ask participants to identify, then make a list of the coaching roles that have been recorded on the flip chart. Distribute "The Ten Roles of Coaches" and ask participants to read the handout carefully. Lead a discussion comparing the roles identified on the flip chart and those on the handout. Note that the handout roles were derived from a book by Killion and Harrison (2006), and provide a succinct yet comprehensive review of coaching in schools.

2. **Invite** participants to number themselves 1–10 around the room. Then direct those who are number 1 to meet in a specified location. Continue with remaining numbers. Number the coaching roles on the chart, 1–10. The groups are to find the number of the coaching role that corresponds to the group's number, read and review the role description again, then design a 3–4 minute role-play that demonstrates their role. They should practice this "production" so that it has the best possibility of portraying this role to the other teams.

3. **Invite** each group to make their presentation without announcing the role they are portraying. At its conclusion, the audience is invited to suggest the role of coaching that has been presented. Discuss differing responses, using the role-play and its discussion to point out and clarify the definitions of the roles.

4. **Provide closure** by inviting participants to return to their original seating. They review and discuss with their table groups the handout, "Adult Learning and Implementing New Practice in Classrooms." Then, using information about the roles and implementing new practice, ask the table groups to make a list of talking points that they will use in a 12-minute presentation to the principal and school improvement team about acquiring coaches to support the staff in their implementation efforts. Share across the table groups.

Future Application

Suggest to the groups that they practice their presentations and then seek to deliver their presentation to the principal, the school leadership team, the parent–teacher association, the deputy superintendent for budgets, or other relevant persons.

Notes:

THE TEN ROLES OF COACHES

Role	Time	Function	Knowledge and Skills	Challenges
Resource Provider		As a resource provider, the coach assists teachers with materials, tools, information, etc. to support classroom instruction. The resources provided could be links from the Internet, materials shared from other teachers, wonderful research/articles that are relevant to teacher practices or ideas shared from other colleagues. Oftentimes, providing these resources helps coaches cross the "threshold" into classrooms.		
Data Coach		Coaches are the liaisons between research and practice, helping teachers learn to improve their practices in a reflective supportive setting. As a data coach, the coach organizes and analyzes a school's data, facilitating conversations among the faculty. The coach supports teachers and administrators in using data to improve instruction on all levels.		
Curriculum Specialist		The coach supports teachers by helping with the "what" of teaching. He/she helps teachers use the national, state, and district curriculum standards to plan instruction and assessment. The coach collaborates and supports teachers in using the curriculum to analyze students' strengths and targets areas for improvement. Coaches need to understand how each curriculum is structured, i.e., thematic approaches, etc., and validate the teachers' content expertise. The coach "taps" into the content expertise of the classroom teacher.		
Instructional Specialist		The coach supports teachers by helping with the "how" of teaching. He/she collaborates with teachers in designing instruction to meet the needs of all students. Multiple instructional		

(Continued)

(Continued)

Role	Time	Function	Knowledge and Skills	Challenges
		strategies/processes are shared with teachers. The coach also coordinates with other specialists in the school to provide a seamless approach to the educational processes in the school, supporting the idea that literacy is a process, not content. The coach must maintain confidentiality and be responsive to the "territorial" limitations of teachers' classrooms.		
Mentor		As a mentor, the coach is a critical friend supporting all teachers, novice and experienced. He/she provides guidance and structure where needed, encouraging relationship building among colleagues. A mentor focuses on teachers' strengths, collaborating and discussing common issues of concern and is a shoulder to bounce off ideas and concerns.		
Classroom Supporter		As a classroom supporter, a coach is a co-planner, a coteacher and a feedback provider. The role is varied including co-planning units of study, providing over the shoulder coaching, participating in coteam teaching, modeling lessons, encouraging reflective practices, assisting with small group instruction, helping with assessments, cocreating classroom management techniques which support instruction and facilitating after visitation discussions. The coach helps facilitate discussions resulting in the collaborative, reflective, accountable, self-evaluative and participative practices that support the educational processes of all students and teachers.		
Learning Facilitator		As a learning facilitator, a coach helps coordinate and facilitate learning experiences for school staff. A coach engages teachers in inquiry, collaborates with teachers to determine areas of need and together they design ways to address the issues of concern. Coaches coordinate cross department classroom visitations, organize		

Role	Time	Function	Knowledge and Skills	Challenges
		professional learning communities within and among schools, help manage study groups, design professional development opportunities, arrange lesson study groups, discuss case studies and examine student work. A coach helps provide opportunities for professional growth on all levels.		
School Leader		A coach as a school leader assists and serves on leadership teams within the school. He/she helps bridge the gaps between and among school programs, remaining focused on the school goals. The coach helps align individual goals and school goals in a non-evaluative way. The coach is not an administrator, a district overseer, nor a classroom peer.		
Catalyst for Change		A coach models and facilitates continuous improvement on the classroom and school levels. On many occasions, he/she challenges the status quo, asks questions and facilitates difficult conversations helping to shape the culture of the school. As a catalyst for change, the coach must motivate the teachers and encourage them to "step out of the box," reinforcing their learnings with support. A coach helps teachers retain what they learn through practice and helps teachers transfer/synthesize their learning by co-planning ways to use the information in new settings.		
Mediator		Coaching is widely used in adult learning and professional development as it emphasizes thinking, problem solving, decision making, and personal resourcefulness to support self-directedness. The coach acts as a mediator, using questioning strategies to assist others to work through ideas by planning, reflecting, and problem-solving. The coach is not the expert providing solutions or answers.		

Source: Chart of the 10 Coaching Roles. Adapted from "Taking the Lead" by Joellen Killion & Cindy Harrison, *Taking the Lead: New Roles for Teachers and School-Based Coaches*, 2006. Reprinted with permission of the National Staff Development Council, www.nsdc.org. All rights reserved.

ADULT LEARNING AND IMPLEMENTING NEW PRACTICE IN CLASSROOMS

Why Coaching

From the mid-seventies to the mid-eighties, Gene Hall and Shirley Hord worked with a team of researchers whose purpose was to study the process of changing educators' practice. In study sites across the nation and beyond, this team interacted with central office personnel, campus-based principals, and teachers K–College. The result of this more-than-a-decade of work was the identification of strategies necessary to implement new practice and the concepts and their measurement tools to aid in the process. These outcomes included the description of Stages of Concern, Levels of Use, and Innovation Configurations (see Hord and Sommers, 2008, pp. 117–130).

These ideas and their measurement tools enabled school leaders/change facilitators to understand the implementers' feelings and behaviors, but also to precisely observe what the implementers were putting into practice and how. Also identified were six strategies found to be imperative for moving new programs, processes, practices, etc. into the classroom or the school's operation (Hall & Hord, 2006, pp. 188–195).

Similarly, a decade later, research done by Bruce Joyce and Beverly Showers (Joyce & Showers, 2002) focused on staff development activities and their effects. Both lines of research identified the importance of adult learning in order to implement new practices in classrooms, and each set of research results noted the significance of one-to-one or small group follow up with the implementers, subsequent to large group learning sessions (typically the format of staff development). This "follow up," (Joyce & Showers, 2002) or "providing continued assistance" (Hall & Hord, 2006) stimulated the now widespread practice of providing coaches to implementers. These coaches provide support to implementers in transferring large group learning to its application in classrooms, where it can benefit students.

What Do Coaches Do?

The idea of coaching has become ubiquitous—everyone is doing it, or so it is claimed. There is a wide variety of coaching, starting with the notion of athletic coaches. In this environment, even champions continue to engage the services of coaches in order to continuously improve their "game" (example: Tiger Woods).

In the educational sector, coaching typically focuses on supporting principals in their leadership roles, and on teachers in implementing new curriculum (content) or instructional strategies. Killion and Harrison (2006) have identified ten roles in the educational context that coaches can enact: resource provider, data coach, curriculum specialist, instructional specialist, mentor, classroom supporter, learning facilitator, school leader, catalyst for change, and mediator—definitions of these roles by Killion and Harrison are found on pages 197–199.

Who Are the Coaches and When Do They Coach?

Coaches can be most anyone who has developed the technical and interpersonal skills required of this role. Because interaction is at the individual or small group level, interpersonal skills are highly important. While there are some persons who have broad content knowledge and excellent instructional skills, these are doomed if the potential coach cannot interact positively and productively with others. This learning opportunity is too brief for in-depth information about coaching, but it can sufficiently inform individuals in order to make a decision about becoming a coach.

An important question is "When will you do the coaching?" Some school districts and/or schools have secured funding that allows the hiring of individuals to spend 100% of their time in the coaching role. Some schools have identified "teachers on special leave" who spend half, or other amounts, of their time devoted to coaching. Some teachers, on a grade-level team or academic department team, coach each other, organizing this work in an invitational and informal way. Budgets, of course, will dictate the amount of time, personnel, and resources provided for coaching. The support by coaches can significantly enhance staff learning and its transfer to classrooms.

Notes:

LEARNING OPPORTUNITY 6.4

Reflection Protocols

Adults do not learn from experience, they learn from processing the experience.

—Judy Arin-Krupp

Outcome

Learners will implement reflection as part of their PLC processes. They will use Reflection-for-Action protocols to help plan learning opportunities and use Reflection-on-Action protocols to help review and process learning opportunities.

Assumption

In the fast-paced world of education, the focus is on getting things done. This is good (for some things) because people want results. The research on reflection shows that higher success rates come from reflection.

There are two kinds of reflection that will be addressed in this learning opportunity. The first is Reflection-for-Action. Think about this in terms of reflecting forward, what is the goal and how will we get there. We are reflecting forward in order to take action.

The second kind of reflection is Reflection-on-Action. This involves reviewing what has happened, what worked, what didn't work as well as we wanted, and how we will change the learning or the process to get to our goal the next time. Depending on the desired outcome of the group or individual conversation, use the appropriate reflection protocol to help facilitate planning forward or reflecting on the learning opportunities, events, or meetings.

Suggested Time

1–1.5 hours

Materials

- Flip chart and markers
- The school's student or staff performance data
- "Reflection Protocols" (see p. 204; one copy for each participant)

Learning Event

1. **Setting the stage:** Ask participants to express their understanding of the outcome desired for the learning event. Ask for elaboration and specificity of the outcome.

2. **Describe** what success of accomplishing the outcome looks like or sounds like. (The more specific the language used, the more likely the PLC will achieve the outcome).

3. **Create** multiple ways of achieving the outcome. By remaining open to possibilities, the group will generate more options than prematurely deciding on one right way. The group builds more trust by not rushing to judgment, by hearing from many sources, and by developing alternative plans in case the one way doesn't work.

4. **Provide closure** by identifying indicators of whether the group is moving toward or away from the outcome. This is a way to develop formative assessments. Knowing these mid-course indicators provides an opportunity to modify the learning event.

Note: The same process can be used for Reflection-on-Action to review, evaluate, and make corrections for future events.

Future Application

What other resources on reflection are there to expand applications? How might we use Reflection-for-Action in other venues, presentations, and events in the school and community? How might using the Reflection-on-Action protocol be used after administrative team meetings, committee work, and with other groups in which we are members?

Notes:

REFLECTION PROTOCOLS

Four-Step Process for Guiding Reflection-for-Action

1. What do you want to accomplish? (goal)

2. What will success look like or sound like? (indicators of success)

3. What are some of the ways that will lead you to your outcome? (strategies)

4. What will be the evidence you are achieving your outcome? (assessment)

Four-Step Process for Guiding Reflection-on-Action

1. What happened? How do you think it went? (description)

2. What might have caused this to happen? (ideas, analysis, data)

3. So what did you learn that you will do again? What did you learn *not* to do again? (meaning, interpretation)

4. Now what? What will you do as a result of reflecting on the event? (implications for action, application)

Notes:

From York-Barr, J., Sommers, W. A., Ghere, G., & Montie, J. (2006). *Reflective Practice to Improve Schools.* Thousand Oaks, CA: Corwin Press. Protocols used with permission of Corwin Press.

LEARNING OPPORTUNITY 6.5

Video Sharing Protocol

Teachers in a learning community are not "inserviced." Instead, they engage in continuous inquiry about teaching. They are researchers, students of teaching, who observe others teach, have others observe them, talk about teaching, and help other teachers. In short, they are professionals.

—Barth (1990)

Outcome

PLC members will provide friendly feedback from a videotaped lesson to improve student learning.

Assumption

Often, while teaching, we can get caught up in the content of a lesson and may not be able to see ourselves or others during the delivery of the lesson. By sharing a video segment of our lesson within the PLC, we are able to step "out" of the teaching moment and observe through a different lens.

Suggested Time

25–30 Minutes

Materials

- Video clip of a lesson
- "Video Sharing Protocol" (see p. 207; one copy for each participant)

Learning Event

1. **Set the stage** by inviting PLC members to discuss the meaning behind Roland Barth's quote found at the top of this page. What is the implication of this quote in regard to learning within the PLC?

2. **Watch** an 8–10 minute video clip of a lesson taught by one of the PLC members. The member, who is sharing his or her teaching, chooses two specific areas in the **Video Sharing Protocol,** *Dimensions of Teaching* where he or she would especially like feedback from PLC members.

3. **Gather** data or evidence on any dimension of teaching that would be helpful feedback, especially the two areas identified by the person sharing the video. Members list the things the students were able to do well and reflect on possible changes and next steps. PLC members might also look for instruction that was helping the students succeed and work toward independence.

4. **Provide closure** by asking members to share what they observed. The sharing might be structured in the following order: (a) affirm what the teacher did well, and (b) identify suggestions for future improvement. You might use the following protocol in the sharing:

> In the video we viewed, I want to affirm
>
> [Teacher's Name] _____'s use of _____.
>
>   o Something I am wondering if you have tried before is _____.
>
>   o As a result of watching the video, a personal learning I am taking away that I want to apply in my own instruction is _____.

Future Application

The PLC might explore other dimensions of effective teaching not identified in this "Video Sharing Protocol" and create a variety of video sharing protocols for giving feedback on classroom instruction.

Notes:

Source: This learning opportunity was submitted by Pam Ryan, who is currently a literacy specialist and coach in District #622, North St. Paul Schools, MN. She spent 3 years employed by the University of Minnesota providing professional development for elementary teachers that focused on strategy instruction and using data to make good instructional choices.

VIDEO SHARING PROTOCOL

Dimensions of Effective Teaching	Question behind the Dimension	I saw . . .	Have you tried . . .
Purpose			
What are students learning?	Is the purpose or outcome for the learning clear to students?		
Student Support Stance			
• Coaching • Modeling • Listening with feedback • Scaffolding	What kind of special support will students need in order to learn?		
Active Responding			
Students are engaged in learning through . . . • reading • writing • hands-on activity • speaking	How am I engaging students to actively participate in the learning?		
Higher-Level Questions or Strategy Instruction			
Is there evidence of inferring, synthesizing, defending thoughts, or of meaningful predicting?	How am I engaging students in higher-level thinking?		
Differentiation			
Is there evidence of differentiation? Are students able to do the work?	What kind of differentiation is needed to support the learning of all students?		

Adapted from the work of Barbara M. Taylor, University of Minnesota.

Part IV
Bringing Closure

Endings and New Beginnings

Our most fervent wish is that the material in this book will challenge and inspire you, surprise you, and provide important new meaning about PLC for you and your colleagues.

In the end, there are no magic bullets, no one right way—there are too many differences and uncontrollable factors. However, we maintain a positive affinity, a hopeful longing for the change and improvement of our schools, and, subsequently, increased successful learning for students. Our premise has been and will continue to be: *to keep hope alive will require learning.*

Einstein said, "Continuing to do the same thing expecting different results is insanity." The one thing we have learned, in our total of over a hundred years of experience, is this: *if it isn't working, try something else.* This requires learning and change. Both will require challenging the status quo, being open to feedback, and being a willing participant in learning. Learning is not a spectator sport.

As Scott Russell Sanders (1998, p. 186) declared, "My search for hope has convinced me that we *can* change our ways of seeing and thinking and living." In order to change our point of view, we have to be open to other points of view. If we had the answers, we would have already taken the steps to make it happen.

To restate what we have said previously, if the PLC becomes a meeting on Tuesday after school, this will be just another program or TLA (three-letter acronym). The goal of the PLC is adult learning. That is our hope. Let us leave you with an acronym for hope, as published in the *Journal of Staff Development* several years ago:

HOPE stands for:

Honesty & **H**umility—We need to be honest about our data, our knowledge and skills, and the results we are getting. We must be humble enough to allow learning to happen, ask for help, and say thank you when others extend our learning.

Options & **O**penness—There are many ways to achieve an outcome. The broader our repertoire, the better able we are to address the multitude of problems. As Angeles Arrien, an anthropologist and author, who makes important contributions to leadership and organizational growth and development, reminds us, be open to outcome, not attached to how to get there.

Patience & **P**ersistence—Patience is not the norm in our culture. Individuals want an answer, and they want it now. If we keep trying with persistence and patiently staying on a learning track, we will find answers. Let's have enough patience to find many right answers.

Efficacy & **E**nthusiasm—We know teacher efficacy is a major driver of student learning. We have to believe we can make a difference. If we don't believe that, we question why we would be in education. We all like to follow people who are positive and have energy to sustain what they are doing. We close with a quote from Angeles Arrien (2002): "If your business is about waking up the dead, GET UP, TODAY IS A WORK DAY!"

Shirley, Jim, and Bill

Resource A

*Excerpt From Hord & Hirsch (2008b, pp. 34–40),
"Making the Promise a Reality"*

The PLC should be considered as two dimensions: one is the encompassing shell that provides the structure within which the second part of the PLC takes place—that is, the work of the PLC. The structural shell (the outer circle in Figure 2.3) includes the following components:——

- The shared values and vision of the participants that guide their work
- The development of shared and supported leadership that involves everyone in decision making about the work of the PLC
- The structural or physical or logistical conditions that support the operations of the PLC
- The relational conditions—the human attitudes and perspectives, and the regard that the members share with each other
- The peer-to-peer support that members give to each other as they observe each other at work and provide feedback

These components sustain the work of the professional learning community as it goes about its self-initiated work. Inside this shell, in its heart and soul, the collective learning that contributes unceasingly to quality teaching and student learning—the important work of the PLC—occurs.

It is here that the staff initiates its work through the examination of a wide array of student performance data to assess the productivity of their teaching, and how those data also indicate the students' needs. In most states, there would be expectations that the staff review the data as it reflects student achievement of the state standards. Many school professional staffs do not understand the true meaning of the state standards and their measurement. In addition, there are many schools where the staff members are not skilled in reviewing data, understanding it, and making sense of it for instructional decision making. There is a strong likelihood that there may be a need for *staff learning* in order to develop the skills we have just noted. Thus a vitally important step is checking to determine if the staff needs professional learning for studying and understanding data and applying it meaningfully.

Figure A.1   Two Dimensions of Professional Learning Communities

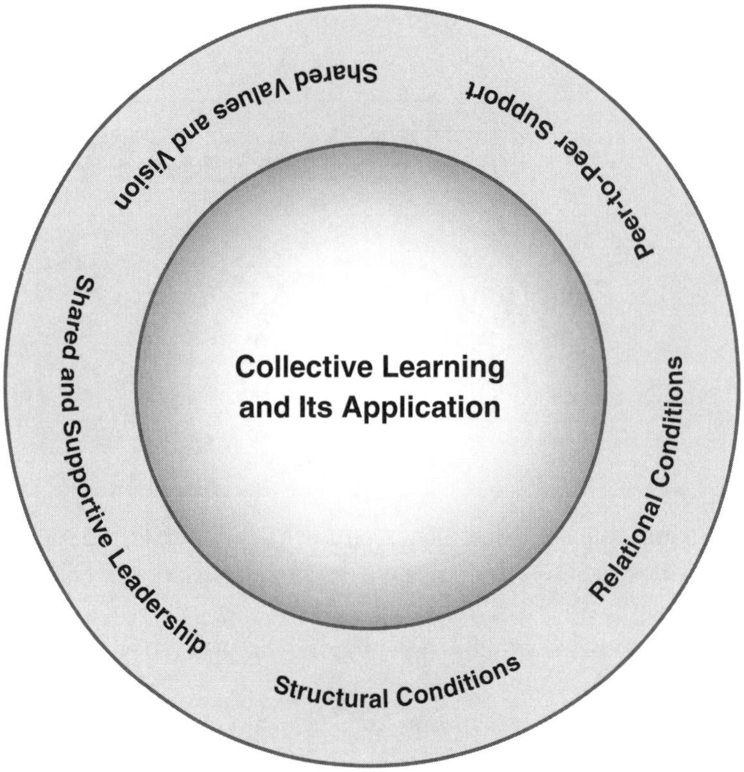

Created by Luis Martinez.

We observe the PLC staff in the details of its work, and note the multiple steps that they employ to conduct their work thoughtfully. (See Figure 2.4 for a simpler description.) It is here that the staff

- *Reflects* on its work for students and related student outcomes as indicated from the data. They evaluate the extent to which their practices and programs are producing the results that they intended.
- *Determines* how well the students are being served (where the staff is succeeding with students' high-quality learning and where it is not so successful) through the study of the data
- *Identifies* student achievement areas in need of attention

Because multiple student needs cannot be addressed simultaneously, the staff also

- *Specifies* priority areas and determines from the data those in need of immediate attention
- *Engages* in studying solutions for the needed areas in order to make decisions about the adoption of new practices or programs. As the staff

members broadly explore the most relevant and powerful means for addressing students' needs, they may well require *professional learning* in order to learn about and develop robust criteria for use in selecting new approaches or programs to use in their classrooms. The fact that a school in the next community is using a particular program is not necessarily the best reason for adopting it (Datnow, 1999).

- *Accepts* the need for *staff learning* in order to implement and employ new knowledge and practices effectively
- *Determines* what they will learn and how they will engage in their new professional learning, and *participates* in ongoing learning in order to become proficient with the identified new programs, practices, content, or instructional strategies
- *Plans* collegially for implementing the new learning and then pursues implementation. There is an array of planning templates; staff would be well advised to *study and learn* about their advantages and disadvantages before determining which to use.
- *Revisits* and *analyzes* the plans and the implementation of the plans with colleagues to assess their success with students. Because this kind of analysis may be new for the staff, *learning* about how to do this may be needed.
- *Revises* or *adjusts* where necessary. With adjustments may come the need for additional *professional learning* about them. With these adjustments and the appearance of new staff learning needs related to student needs, the PLC cycle of improvement continues.

These steps overlap a great deal with each other; some of them are easily integrated with others (see Figure 2.4). The steps of the process may be used with issues and problem solving other than increasing students' academic learning. As one example, we have seen a professional learning community at the high school level use these steps when challenged by the school board to consider the matter of schoolwide uniforms for students. The staff collected and referred to data, focused on specific issues, and did research to expand their knowledge base and understanding of the factors involved in the issue of school uniforms. They undertook an extensive learning agenda to better understand the students' and adults' points of view about the matter and what impact it might have on the school's culture of learning and on students' academic performance. It was a significant learning experience for the staff, and enabled them to make a more authentic and appropriate recommendation to the board.

> Too often, unfortunately, little care is taken to provide staff development that ensures staff members develop deep understanding of content and skills for using new practices.

More often than not, in the typical school improvement process, the staff's learning of new programs and practices is taken for granted. Too often, unfortunately, little care is taken to provide staff development that ensures staff members develop deep understanding of content and skills for using new practices. Such lackluster efforts typically result in the superficial use of new practices and programs. A culture of

Figure A.2 The Work of the Professional Learning Community

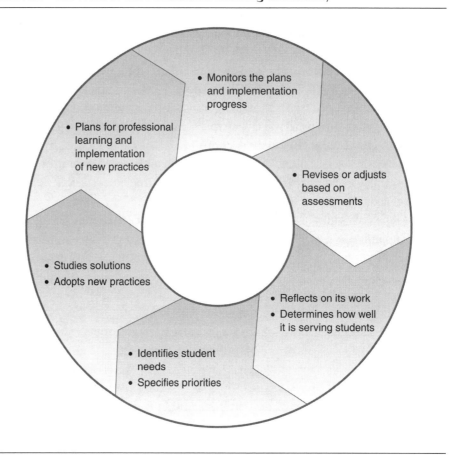

- Monitors the plans and implementation progress
- Plans for professional learning and implementation of new practices
- Revises or adjusts based on assessments
- Studies solutions
- Adopts new practices
- Reflects on its work
- Determines how well it is serving students
- Identifies student needs
- Specifies priorities

Created by Luis Martinez.

appearance develops, in which individuals conform but don't reform—and the results promised by new programs are never realized. *Too often, unfortunately, little care is taken to provide staff development that ensures staff members develop deep understanding of content and skills for using new practices.*

Do not think that PLCs are immune to this distressing and too-common phenomenon. A superficial attention to the work and to the staff's learning would doom any such initiative. As in all change efforts, leaders who act vigorously to maintain the focus have the power to contribute greatly to successful change efforts. Creating and employing the PLC model is most certainly a change for a staff. The likelihood for deeper learning is increased by the thoughtful and consistent attention to the structures and resources that support the PLC, and to the monitoring of the PLC's work by the principal and other leaders—of the small-group teams and the whole school community. There is nothing magical in the PLC structure; rather, its success is determined by the degree to which its members commit to the goal of student learning and embrace their respective roles and responsibilities. That crucial factor is what assures high-quality work. Its effectiveness depends on individuals engaging in the learning and work that the community has determined for itself. When a PLC staff has focused its energies on student benefits, its commitment to the identified student goals encourages staff members in their study and work. This commitment by the whole staff reinforces and motivates the work of the individuals.

Because all change and improvement is dependent on learning, the professional learning community is a structure and way of working that provides the environment in which principals and teachers set about intentionally learning in order to increase their effectiveness—and, subsequently, increase student results. When only *some* staff members engage in individual professional learning, only *some* students will benefit. When *all* staff members engage in PLCs, *all* students benefit. The goal of our schools must be the regular engagement of all educators in professional learning communities

- Where ongoing learning and application of learning is nonnegotiable
- Where goals are established for the entire school, and responsibility is assumed at all levels
- Where acknowledging needs is a sign of strength rather than weakness
- Where teachers recognize that their learning is directly tied to their students' learning
- Where entire faculties have numerous opportunities for celebration of working in the same direction and producing great results for students

REFERENCES

Boyd, V., & Hord, S. M. (1994a). *Principals and the new paradigm: Schools as learning communities.* Paper presented at the annual meeting of the American Educational Research Association, New Orleans.

Boyd, V., & Hord, S. M. (1994b). Schools as learning communities. *Issues . . . About Change, 4*(1). Datnow, A. (1999). *How schools choose externally developed reform designs* (Report No. 35). Baltimore: Center for Research on the Education of Students Placed at Risk.

DuFour, R., Eaker, R., & DuFour, R. (2005). *On common ground: The power of professional learning communities.* Bloomington, IN: Solution Tree.

Gonzalez, C. E., Resta, P. E., & De Hoyos, M. L. (2005). *Barriers and facilitators on implementation of policy initiatives to transform higher education teaching-learning process.* Paper presented at the annual meeting of the American Educational Research Association, Montreal.

Hall, G. E., & Hord, S. M. (2006). *Implementing change: Patterns, principles, and potholes* (2nd ed.). Boston: Pearson/Allyn & Bacon.

Hargreaves, A. (2003). *Teaching in the knowledge society: Education in the age of insecurity.* New York: Teachers College Press.

Hargreaves, A., & Fink, D. (2006). *Sustainable leadership.* San Francisco: Jossey-Bass.

Hord, S. M. (Ed.). (2004). *Learning together, leading together: Changing schools through professional learning communities.* New York: Teachers College Press.

Louis, K. S., Marks, H. M., & Kruse, S. (1996, Winter). Teachers' professional community in restructuring schools. *American Educational Research Journal, 33*(4), 757–798.

McLaughlin, M. W., & Talbert, J. E. (2006). *Building school-based teacher learning communities: Professional strategies to improve student achievement.* New York: Teachers College Press.

National Association of Elementary School Principals. (2004). *Leading learning communities: NAESP standards for what principals should know and be able to do.* Alexandria, VA: Author.

National Staff Development Council. (2001). *Standards for staff development: Advancing student learning through staff development.* Oxford, OH: Author.

Time: Find it, save it, stretch it, reshape it. (2007, Spring). *Journal of Staff Development, 28*(2).

Time for adult learning. (1999, Spring). *Journal of Staff Development, 20*(2).

References

Adams, M. G. (2004). *Change your questions, change your life.* New York: Ballantine.

Adler, R., & Towne, N. (2002). *Looking out/Looking in* (10th ed.). New York: Harcourt Brace.

Alig-Mielcarek, J., & Hoy, W. K. (2005). Instructional leadership: Its nature, meaning, and influence. In W. K. Hoy & C. Miskel (Eds.). *Educational leadership and reform* (pp. 29–54). Greenwich, CT: Information Age Publishers.

Arrien, A. (2002, July 12). Quote. Triumph of Imagination Workshop. Riverwood Conference, Minneapolis, MN.

Bandura, A. (1977). Self-efficacy: Toward a unifying theory of behavioral change. *Psychological Review, 84,* 191–215.

Bandura, A. (1977). *Social learning theory.* Englewood Cliffs, N.J.: Prentice-Hall.

Bandura, A. (1993). Perceived self-efficacy in cognitive development and functioning. *Educational Psychologist, 28,* 117–48.

Bandura, A. (1997). *Self-efficacy: The exercise of control.* New York: Freeman.

Barth, R. S. (1980). *Run school run.* Cambridge, MA: Harvard University.

Barth, R. S. (1984). Sandboxes and honeybees. *Education Week,* May 1.

Bolam, R., McMahon, A., Stoll, L., Thomas, S., Wallace, M., Hawkey, K. & Greenwood, A. (2005). *Creating and sustaining effective professional learning communities.* DFES Research Report RR637. University of Bristol. Retrieved March 2008, from www.dfes.gov.uk/ research/data/upload files/RR637.pdf (research report) and www.dfes.giv.uk/research/data/uploadfiles/RB637.pdf (research brief).

Bloom B. S. (1956). *Taxonomy of educational objectives, handbook I: The cognitive domain.* New York: David McKay Co., Inc.

Bryk, A. S., & Schneider, B. (2002). *Trust in schools: A core resource for improvement.* New York: Russell Sage.

Collins, J. (2001). *Good to great.* New York: HarperCollins.

Costa and Kallick (2009). *Habits of mind across the curriculum: Practical and creative strategies for teachers.* Alexandria, VA: Association for Supervision and Curriculum Development.

Covey, S. (1989). *The 7 habits of highly effective people.* New York: Freepress.

Csikszentmihalyi, M. (2004). *Good business: Leadership, flow, and the making of meaning.*

Cunningham, W., & Gresso, D. (1993). *Cultural leadership: The culture of excellence in education.* Needham Heights, Massachusetts: Allyn and Bacon.

Deal, T. E., & Kennedy, A. A. (1982). *Corporate cultures.* Reading, MA: Addison Wesley.

Deal, T. E., & Peterson, K. D. (1998). *Shaping school culture: The heart of leadership.* San Francisco: Jossey-Bass.

Dweck, C. S. (2006). *Mindset: The new psychology of success.* Somerville, MA: Wisdom.

Edwards, J. L., & And, O. (1996). *Factor and rasch analysis of the school culture survey.* Paper presented at the Annual Meeting of the American Educational Research Association (New York, NY, April 8–12, 1996).

Epstein, J. L. (1989). Family structure and student motivation. In R. E. Ames & C. Ames (Eds.), *Research on motivation in education: Vol. 3. Goals and cognitions* (pp. 259–295). New York: Academic Press.

Feltman. C. (2001). *Leadership and the enemies of learning.* Retrieved February 19, 2007, from http://www.insightcoaching.com/insights-papers.html

Garmston, R. (2007, November). Collaborative culture. *Journal of Staff Development* (28)1, 69–70. Retrieved July 30, 2009 from http://www.nsdc.org/news/articleDetails.cfm?articleID=1354)

Garmston, R., & Wellman, B. (2009). *The adaptive school, a sourcebook for developing collaborative groups.* 2nd ed. Norwood, MA: Christopher-Gordon.

Gharajedaghi, J. (2006). *Systems thinking: Managing chaos and complexity.* San Diego, CA: Butterworth-Heinemann.

Goddard, R. D., Hoy, W. K., & Woolfolk Hoy, A. (2000). Collective teacher efficacy: Its meaning, measure, and impact on student achievement. *American Educational Research Journal, 37,* 479–508.

Goddard, R. D., Hoy, W. K., & Woolfolk Hoy, A. (2004). Collective efficacy: Theoretical development, empirical evidence, and future directions. *Educational Researcher, 33,* 3–13.

Goddard, R. D., LoGerfo, L., & Hoy, W. K. (2004). High school accountability: The role of collective efficacy. *Educational Policy 18*(30), 403–425.

Goddard, R. D., Sweetland, S. R., & Hoy, W. K. (2000). Academic emphasis of urban elementary schools and student achievement: a multi-level analysis. *Educational Administration Quarterly, 36,* 692–701.

Goddard, R. D., Tschannen-Moran, M., & Hoy, W, K. (2001). Teacher trust in students and parents: A multilevel examination of the distribution and effects of teacher trust in urban elementary schools. *Elementary School Journal, 102,* 3–17.

Goldsmith, M. (2007). Bad behavior. Retrieved July 28, 2009, from www.marshall goldsmithlibrary.com/cim/articles_display.php?aid=363

Greenspan, S. I., & Shanker, S. (2006). *The first idea: How symbols, language, and intelligence evolved from our primate ancestors to modern humans.* Cambridge, MA: Da Capo Press.

Hall, G. E., & Hord, S. M. (2006). *Implementing change: Patterns, principles, and potholes.* Boston: Allyn & Bacon.

Hinton, R. (1966). *Fanshen,* New York: Vintage.

Hirsh, S., & Hord, S. (2008). Leader and learner, *Principal Leadership, 9*(4), 26–30.

Hord, S. M. (1997). Professional learning communities: What are they and why are they important? *Issues . . . about Change 6*(1), 5–6.

Hord, S. M. (2007). Learn in community with others. *Journal of Staff Development, 28*(3), 39–40.

Hord, S. M., & Hirsh, S. (2008). Making the promise a reality. In A. M. Blankstein, P. D. Houston, & R. W. Cole (Eds.), *Sustaining professional learning communities* (pp. 36–38). Thousand Oaks, CA: Corwin.

Hord, S. M., Rutherford, W. L., Huling-Austin, L., & Hall, G. E. (2004). *Taking charge of change.* Austin, TX: SEDL.

Hord, S. M., & Sommers, W. A. (2008). *Leading professional learning communities, Voices from research and practice.* Thousand Oaks, CA: Corwin.

Hoy, W. K. (2002). Faculty trust: A key to student achievement. *Journal of School Public Relations, 23*(2) 88–103.

Hoy, W. K., & Hannum, J. (1997). Middle school climate: An empirical assessment of organizational health and student achievement. *Educational Administration Quarterly, 33,* 290–311.

Hoy, W. K., & Sabo, D. J. (1998). *Quality middle schools: Open and healthy.* Thousand Oaks, CA: Corwin.

Hoy, W. K., Sweetland, S. R., & Smith, P. A. (2002). Toward an organizational model of achievement in high schools: The significance of collective efficacy. *Educational Administration Quarterly, 38,* 77–93.

Hoy, W. K., & Tarter, C. J. (2004). *Administrators solving the problems of practice: Decision-making concepts, cases, and consequences.* Boston: Allyn & Bacon.

Hoy, W. K., Tarter, C. J., & Bliss, J. (1990). Organizational climate, school health, and effectiveness. *Educational Administration Quarterly, 26,* 260–279.

Hoy, W. K., Tarter, C. J., & Kottkamp, R. B. (1991). *Open schools/healthy schools: Measuring organizational climate.* Beverly Hills, CA: Sage.

Hoy, W. K., Tarter, C. J., & Woolfolk Hoy, A. (2006a). Academic optimism of schools: A force for student achievement. *American Educational Research Journal, 43,* 425–446.

Hoy, W. K., Tarter, C. J., & Woolfolk Hoy, A. (2006b). Academic optimism of schools. In Wayne K. Hoy & Cecil Miskel (eds.). *Contemporary issues in educational policy and school outcomes* (pp. 135–156). Greenwich, CN: Information Age.

Hoy, W. K., & Miskel, C. G. (2005). *Educational administration: Theory, research, and practice* (7th ed.). New York: McGraw-Hill.

Hoy, W. K., & Tschannen-Moran, M. (1999). Five faces of trust: An empirical confirmation in urban elementary schools. *Journal of School Leadership, 9,* 184–208.

Hoy, W. K., & Tschannen-Moran, M. (2003). The conceptualization and measurement of faculty trust in schools. In W. K. Hoy & C. Miskel (Eds.), *Studies in leading and organizing schools* (pp. 181-207). Greenwich, CT: Information Age.

Hultman, K. (2006). *Values-driven change: Strategies and tools for long-term success.* Lincoln, NE: iUniverse.

Joyce, B., & Showers, B. (2002). *Student achievement through staff development* (3rd ed.). Alexandria, VA: ASCD.

Joyce, B., & Weil, M. (1980). *Models of teaching.* Englewood Cliffs, NJ: Prentice Hall.

Kegan, R. (1982). *The evolving self: Problem and process in human development.* Cambridge, MA: Harvard University Press.

Killion, J., & Harrison, C. (2006). *Taking the lead: New roles for teachers and school-based coaches.* Oxford, OH: National Staff Development Council.

Kolb, D. (1984). *Experiential learning.* Cliffs, NJ: Prentice-Hall.

Lane, C. (n.d.). *Bloom's taxonomy: In the distance learning technology resource guide.* The Education Coalition. Retrieved January 11, 2007, from http://www.tecweb.org/eddevel/edtech/blooms.html

Lencioni, P. (2004). *Death by meeting.* San Francisco, CA: Jossey-Bass.

Lewin, K. (1951). *Field theory in social sciences.* New York: Harper & Row.

Lezotte, L., & McKee, K. M. (2002). *Assembly required: A continuous school improvement system.* Okemos, MI: Effective Schools Products.

Lightfoot, S. (1983). *Good high schools: Portraits of character and culture.* New York: Basic.

Little, J. W. (1981). *School success and staff development in urban desegregated schools: A summary of recently completed research.* Paper presented at the annual meeting of the American Education Research Association, Los Angeles, April.

Lortie, D. C. (1972). *School teacher.* Chicago: University of Chicago.

Loucks, S. F. (1983). At last: Some good news from a study of school Improvement. *Educational Leadership, 41* (November): 4–9.

Louis, K. S., & Kruse, S. D. (1995). *Professionalism and community: Perspectives on reforming urban schools.* Thousand Oaks, CA: Corwin.

McCarthy, B. (2000). *About learning.* Wauconda, IL: About Learning.

McCarthy, B., & O'Neill-Blackwell, J. (2007). *Hold on, you lost me!* Alexandria, VA: ASTD Press.

Olalla, J. (2004). *From knowledge to wisdom: Essays on the crisis in contemporary learning.* Boulder, CO: Newfield Network, Inc.

Orem, S., Binkert, J., Clancy, A., (2007). *Appreciative coaching.* San Francisco: Jossey-Bass.

Pajares, F. (1994). Role of self-efficacy and self-concept beliefs in mathematical problem-solving: A path analysis. *Journal of Educational Psychology, 86,* 193–203.

Pajares, F. (1997). Current directions in self-efficacy research.

Patterson, K., Grenny, J., Maxfield, D., McMillan, R., Switzler, A. (2008). *Influencer.* New York: McGraw-Hill.

Peat, F. D., (2008). *Gentle action, bringing creative change to a turbulent world.* Grosseto, Italy: Pari.

Peters, T. J., & Waterman, R. H. Jr. (1982). *In search of excellence.* New York, Harper & Row.

Peterson, C. (2000). The future of optimism. *American Psychologist, 55,* 44–55.

Pintrich, P. R., & Schunk, D. H. (2002). *Motivation in education: Theory, research, and applications* (2nd ed.). Upper Saddle River, NJ: Merrill/Prentice-Hall.

Purkey, S. C., & Smith, M. S. (1982). Too soon to cheer? Synthesis of research on effective schools *Educational Leadership, 41* (December), 64–69.

Richardson, J. (1998). Student learning grows in professional cultures. *Tools for Schools* (August/September). National Staff Development Council.

Sanders, S. (1998). *Hunting for hope.* Boston: Beacon Press.

Saphier, J. (1989). *The school culture survey.* Acton, MA: Research for Better Teaching.

Saphier, J., & King, M. (1985). Good seeds grow in strong cultures. *Educational Leadership, 42*(6).

Saphier, J. D., & Gower, R. (1982). *The skillful teacher.* Carlisle, MA: Research for Better Teaching.

Scott, S. (2002). *Fierce conversations: Achieving success at work and in life, one conversation at a time.* New York: Penguin Putnam.

Seashore, K., Anderson, A. R., & Riedel, E. (2003). *Implementing arts for academic achievement: The impact of mental models, professional community and interdisciplinary teaming.* Paper prepared for Minneapolis Public Schools, University of Minnesota, CAREI, and presented at the annual conference of the International Congress for School Effectiveness and Improvement, Rotterdam, Netherlands, January.

Senge, P., (2000). *Schools that learn.* New York: Doubleday-Dell.

Sergiovanni, T. (1984). Leadership and excellence in schooling. *Educational Leadership, 41* (February), 4–13.

Sitkin, S. B., & Roth, N. L. (1993). Explaining the limited effectiveness of legalistic remedies for trust/distrust. *Organization Science, 4*(3), 367–392.

Smith, P. A., Hoy, W. K., & Sweetland, S. R. (2001). Organizational health of high schools and dimensions of faculty trust. *Journal of School Leadership, 11,* 135–151.

Snyder, C. R., Shorey, H. S., Cheavens, J., Pulvers, K. M., Adams, V. H. III, & Wiklund, C. (2002). Hope and academic success in college. *Journal of Educational Psychology, 94,* 820–826.

Solomon, R., & Flores, F. (2001). *Building trust: In business, politics, relationships, and life.* New York: Oxford University.

Spillane, J. (2006). *Distributed leadership.* San Francisco: Jossey-Bass.

Stoll, L., & Louis, K. S. (2007). *Professional learning communities: Divergence, depth and dilemmas.* Columbus, OH: Open University Press.

Straus, D. (2002). *How to make collaboration work.* San Francisco: Berrett-Koehler Publishers.

Taylor, B. M., Pearson, P. D., Peterson, D. P., & Rodriguez, M. C. (2005). The CIERA School Change Framework: An evidence-based approach to professional development and school reading improvement. *Reading Research Quarterly, 40*(1), 40–69.

Tschannen-Moran, M., & Hoy, W. K. (2000). A multidisciplinary analysis of the nature, meaning, and measurement of trust. *Review of Educational Research, 70,* 547–93.

Tschannen-Moran, M. (2004). *Trust matters: Leadership for successful schools.* San Francisco, CA: Jossey-Bass.

Tschannen-Moran, M., Woolfolk Hoy, A. W., & Hoy, W. K. (1998). Teacher efficacy: Its meaning and measure. *Review of Educational Research, 68,* 202–248.

Vella, J. (2008). *On teaching and learning: Putting the principles and practices of dialogue education into action.* San Francisco: Jossey-Bass.

Von Frank, V. (Ed.). (2008). *Finding time for professional learning.* Oxford, OH: National Staff Development Council.

Vygotsky, L. S. (1978). *Mind in society.* (M. Cole, V. John-Steiner, S. Scribner, & E. Souberman, Eds.). Cambridge, MA: Harvard University Press.

Wagner, C. R. (2006). The school leader's tool for assessing and improving school culture, *Principal Leadership 7*(4), 41–44.

Weisbord, M., & Janoff, S. (2007). *Don't just do something, stand there! Ten principles for leading meetings that matter.* San Francisco: Berrett-Koehler.

Wheatley (1996)

Index

CORWIN

A SAGE Company

The Corwin logo—a raven striding across an open book—represents the union of courage and learning. Corwin is committed to improving education for all learners by publishing books and other professional development resources for those serving the field of PreK–12 education. By providing practical, hands-on materials, Corwin continues to carry out the promise of its motto: **"Helping Educators Do Their Work Better."**